HEALING MANTRAS
Sacred Words of Power

Other similar **INDIGO BOOKS** available (or to be published shortly) are:

VRATA. SACRED VOWS AND TRADITIONAL FASTS, M. N. Dutt

AN INTRODUCTION TO YOGA, Annie Besant

OCCULT PRINCIPLES OF HEALTH AND HEALING, Max Heindel

YOUR FORCES AND HOW TO USE THEM

HYPNOSIS FOR BEGINNERS, Dylan Morgan

MEDICAL ASTROLOGY. A GUIDE TO HEALING. A TREATISE ON ASTRO-DIAGNOSIS FROM THE HOROSCOPE AN HAND, Max Meindel & A. F. Heindel

THE POWER OF CONCENTRATION, Theron Q. Dumont

HEALING MANTRAS. SACRED WORDS OF POWER, M. N. Dutt

available from COSMO

ENCYCLOPAEDIA OF TANTRA, in 5 volumes by Sadhu Santideva

RITUALS AND PRACTICES OF TANTRA, in 3 volumes by Gaurinath Sastri

INTRODUCTION TO TANTRA, in 2 volumes by Gaurinath Sastri

ENCYCLOPAEDIA OF BUDDHIST TANTRA, in 5 volumes by Sadhu Santideva

For getting information on our forthcoming books please write to us.

HEALING MANTRAS
Sacred Words of Power

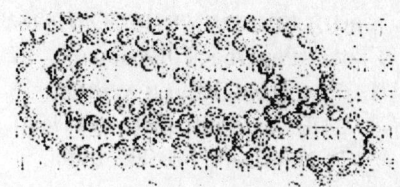

Manmatha Nath Dutt
Other similar books by the author
GARUDA PURANA; AGNI PURANA; MATASYA PURANA

INDIGO BOOKS

An
INDIGO BOOK
PUBLISHED BY INDIGO BOOKS
Paperback division of
COSMO PUBLICATIONS,
24-B, Ansari Road, Darya Ganj,
New Delhi 110 002, India.

INDIGO BOOKS and
COSMO PUBLICATIONS
are wholly owned subsidiaries of
GENESIS PUBLISHING PVT. LTD.,
New Delhi, India

HEALING MANTRAS. SACRED WORDS OF POWER

Copyright © 2002 INDIGO BOOKS

First Published 2002

ISBN 81-292-0017-1

This book is sold subject to the condition that it shall not, by way of trade or otherwise, be lent, re-sold, hired out or otherwise circulated without the publisher's prior consent in any form of binding or cover other than that in which this is published and without a similar condition including this condition being imposed on the subsequent purchaser.

ALL RIGHTS RESERVED

PRINTED AND BOUND IN INDIA

Contents

	Introduction	i
I	The Mantra which is irresistible in the Three Worlds	1
II	The incantation for obtaining victories in the Three Worlds	3
III	The six sorts of Charms	7
IV	The Medicinal or Curative incantations	10
V	Trikhandi Mantras	14
VI	The most mysterious of the sin expiating rites	23
VII	The Omkar Mantra	28
VIII	The Gayatri Mantra	34
IX	The use of the Gayatri Mantra for worshipping the phalic emblem	37
X	The Mantras to be used on the occasion of the installation of a king	39
XI	The Rites Mantras of the Sama Veda	45
XII	The Rites and Mantras of the Atharvan Veda	48
XIII	How to ward off the dreadful visitations of Nature	52
XIV	The ablution for exorcising the malignant spirit Vinayaka	56

XV	Maheswara Ablution	58
XVI	The Mantras for consecrating the royal umbrella	62
XVII	The incantation of Vishnu Panjaram	67
XVIII	The two division of the Vedic Mantras	69
XIX	The Mantras which grant all creature comforts	71
XX	The Mantras destroying the baneful influences of malignant Stars	78
XXI	The Principal Mantras sacred to the lord of heaven	85
XXII	The Mantras sacred to the god Shiva	90
XXIII	The recitation of The fifty names of Vishnu	95
XXIV	The incantation for stupefying the faculties of adversaries	98
XXV	The Mantras by which the Three Worlds can be enchanted	102
XXVI	The Mantram sacred to the goddess of Fortune	108
XXVII	The Mantra for worshipping the goddess Tvarita who grants enjoyment of earthly comforts and salvation after death	113
XXVIII	The worship of the goddess Tvarita by which one can enjoy all comforts in this life	117
XXIX	The incantations by which one can acquire Learning	124
XXX	The Mantras for the goddess Tvarita	128
XXXI	The Mantras for realising one's all desires	131
XXXII	The Prasada Mantra of Shiva	133

XXXIII	The Same Mantra (Continued)	137
XXXIV	The ceremony of Astra-Yajnam	140
XXXV	The bliss of the same Mantra	143
XXXVI	The Mantra for curing diseases and warding off death	146
XXXVII	The peace-giving rite of Shiva-Shanti	152
XXXVIII	The Metre of the Divine Gayatri	157
XXXIX	The metre Jagati	158
XL	The metre Utkriti	160
XLI	Mantra cures (curative formulas) of Snake bite as narrated by S'iva	163
XLII	Enumeration of diverse Incantations, Matras (Nana vidya)	166
XLIII	The Hymn to Narasimha	167
XLIV	The Jñánamritam Stotram	170
XLV	The Hymn to Visnu composed by the holy Mārkandeya	174
XLVI	The Hymn to Achyuta	175

INTRODUCTION

MANTRA YOGA: THE POTENCY OF SOUND
The Sonic Universe

Modern science and ancient Tantra agree: The universe is an ocean of energy. Where they differ is in how this fact should be understood. The Tantric approach affirms that this finding has very personal implications. If matter can indeed be resolved to energy, then the human body-as a product of the material cosmos—is likewise energy at a more primary level. As the *Tantras* further insist, energy and consciousness are ultimately conjoined as the two poles of the same Reality, Shiva-Shakti. Therefore the human body is, in the final analysis, not merely unconscious matter but a stepped-down version of superconscious Energy.

This insight has far-reaching practical ramifications for each person. For, if the body is not merely the sarcophagus of an immaterial soul but a vibrant, living reality suffused with the same Consciousness that also animates the mind, then we must cease to regard the body as an external object radically distinct from our conscious selves. The habitual split between body and mind is not only unwarranted but detrimental to the kind of wholeness to which spiritual seekers aspire. To put it in traditional terms, the body is a temple of the Divine. It is the foundation for realizing the essential oneness of everything; it is the jumping-board from which we can attain enlightenment-an enlightenment that for it to be true must necessarily include each of the physical body's thirty billion billion billion cells.

The Tantric position is very clear: Existence is One, and we are it. All division and divisiveness is a subsequent mental construct (*vikalpa*). However, the *Tantras* do not deny differentiation as such. The Many appears within the One but without ever becoming isolated from it. The Tantric adepts merely reject the notion of duality and the accompanying ego-driven attitude of separativeness. Existence is continuity "stretching from the Radical Potential to its actualisation as the crust of matter."[1]

All this is beautifully contained in the concept of the serpent power (*kundalinî-shakti*), which is the ultimate Energy, or Shakti, as it manifests at a suitably stepped-down degree in the human body. The *kundalinî* is the power of Consciousness (*cit-shakti*), and as such is the superintelligent force sustaining the body and the mind through the agency of the life energy (*prâna*). Upon full awakening, the *kundalinî's* fundamental role in the maintenance of our physical and mental structures and functions is witnessed directly. Gopi Krishna has expressed this vividly as follows:

> I searched my brain for an explanation and revolved every possibility in my mind to account for the surprising development as I watched attentively the incredible movement of this intelligent radiation from hour to hour and day to day. At times I was amazed at the uncanny knowledge it displayed of the complicated nervous mechanism and the masterly way in which it darted here and there as if aware of every twist and turn in the body.[2]

That the *kundalinî* is a cosmic—even a supracosmic—intelligent energy is borne out by her traditional name *sarasvatî*, meaning "she who flows." Originally, this was the name of Northern India's mightiest river, which flowed through the heartland of the Vedic civilization, now lying buried under the sand dunes of the Thar Desert. A memory of the former cultural greatness of that region has survived in the figure of Sarasvatî, the Goddess of learning, who is typically portrayed holding a lute (*vînâ*). Shakti is indeed the source of all knowledge and wisdom, for in the absence of the Goddess power, neither the mind nor the brain would exist.

Moreover, in the Tantric scriptures, *vînâ-danda* or "fiddle stick" is an esoteric designation for the spinal column and, by extension, the central channel. When the central channel is activated through the ascent of the life force (*prâna*) followed by the serpent power itself, all kinds of subtle sounds can be heard inwardly. Connected with this is the idea that the body of the divine serpent is composed of the fifty basic letters of the Sanskrit alphabet, which corresponds to the fifty skulls worn by the Goddess Kâlî as a garland (*mâlâ*). The alphabet is called "garland of letters" (*varna-mâlâ*), suggesting the higher purpose envisioned for human language by the Vedic sages, namely to appropriately honor and express divine Reality.

Sanskrit, as the word itself indicates, is a purposely constructed (*samskrita*) language. According to tradition, it is the language of the Gods—*deva-vânî*.[3] The script itself is known as *deva-nâgarî* ("city of the Gods"), which hints at the Tantric (and Vedic) notion that each letter of the alphabet represents a particular type of fundamental energy, or deity power. Together these matrix energies weave the web of cosmic and hence also bodily existence. Here we have again the idea, quintessential to Tantra, that the microcosm mirrors the macrocosm. The body and the universe at large are produced by the same energy equations that the Tantrics have expressed in the form of the fifty principal sounds of the Sanskrit alphabet, which was developed in the context of spiritual practice and sacred vision.

As the *Shâradâ-Tilaka-Tantra* (1.108) states, the *kundalinî* is the sonic Absolute (*shabda-brahman*). The sonic Absolute is the soundless Absolute (*ashabda-brahman*) stepped down to the level of cosmic sound (*shabda*), corresponding to the hermetic "harmony of the spheres" and the gnostic logos: "In the beginning was the Word..." The *Mantra-Yoga-Samhitâ* (3) proffers this explanation:

> Wherever there is activity, it is inevitably connected with vibration. Similarly, wherever there is vibration witnessed in the world it is invariably associated with [audible or inaudible] sound.

Owing to the differentiation occurring at the initial moment, creation is vibratory as well. The sound produced then is the *pranava*, which has the form of the auspicious *om-kâra*.

The *Shâradâ-Tilaka-Tantra* (1.108) describes the cosmogonic process in terms of the production of sound as follows: From the supreme Shakti—pure Consciousness combined with the factor of lucidity (*sattva*)—comes the most subtle sound (*dhvani*), which is marked by a preeminence of the factors of lucidity and dynamism (*rajas*). Out of the *dhvani* develops the subtle sound (*nâda*), characterized by a mixture of the factors of lucidity, dynamism, and inertia (*tamas*). This subtle sound, in turn, gives rise to the energy of restriction (*nirodhikâ*), which has an excess of the factor of inertia. This ontic principle emanates the "half-moon" (*ardha-indu*, written *ardhendu*), which at this lower level again shows a predominance of the factor of lucidity. Out of it comes the vibratory source-point (*bindu*), the immediate source of all letters and words. These form *mantras*, which are thus manifestations or vehicles of Shakti.

This scripture (1.8) further explains that the *bindu* is itself composed of three parts, viz. *nâda, bindu,* and *bîja* ("seed"). The first part has a predominance of Consciousness (i.e., Shiva), the second a preponderance of Energy (i.e., Shakti), and the third an equal presence of Consciousness and Energy. Such esoteric accounts of the evolution of sound remain relatively unintelligible outside of Tantric practice. However, they become increasingly meaningful as the practitioner makes progress on the path of *mantra-vidyâ* or "mantric science."

Unlike the sounds we can hear with our ears, the cosmic sound is uncaused. It is an infinite vibration (*spanda*) that is coextensive with the universe itself and is realizable only in deep meditation when the senses and the mind have been deactivated. The primordial sound is symbolically represented by the sacred syllable *om*. Although not mentioned directly in the *Rig-Veda,* the *om*-sound—also called *pranava*[4] and *udgîtha*—is hinted at in various hymns. It is first mentioned by name in the *Shukla-Yajur-Veda* (1.1).

Later on, in the era of the *Upanishads,* it came to be explained as consisting of the three constituent sounds *a, u,* and *m*. According to the *Mândûkya-Upanishad* (9-12), these represent the three states of waking, dreaming, and sleeping respectively. Beyond these is the "fourth" (*turîya*), which is the condition of utter wakefulness throughout all states of consciousness. It is the ultimate Being-Consciousness itself. Subsequent scriptures have elaborated on this symbolism, adding the elements of *nâda* (subtle sound) and *bindu* (zero-dimensional seed-point).[5] I will address these and other metapsychological refinements in the next section.

The Tantric speculations about sound and transcendence are extremely ancient and were foreshadowed by the Vedic notion of *vâc,* divine speech. In the *Rig-Veda*(10.125.3-5), *vâc* is personified as the Goddess by that name, who utters the following sacred words:

> I am the queen, gatherer of riches, the wise one, chief among those worthy of sacrifice. The deities have placed me in many places, and so I abide in many stations and enter into many [forms].

> Through Me alone, he who eats food sees, breathes, and hears what is said. Dwelling in Me, they perish [ignorant of this fact]. Listen who can hear, I tell you that in which you should have faith.

> Verily, I declare of myself that which is congenial to deities and humans. Whomsoever I desire I render him formidable (*ugra*), a seer, a sage, a *brahmin.*

Another hymn of the *Rig-Veda* (10.71.4) states that "one who looks does not see Vâc, and another who listens does not hear her." She reveals herself, the text continues, as a loving wife reveals her body to the husband. In other words, Vâc is extremely subtle and self-revealing—an agent of grace. As the opening verse declares, it was through affection that Vâc first revealed herself to the Vedic seers. Then, continues verse 3, wise bards traced Vâc's path through their sacrifices and found her hidden within the sages. There can be no question that this Vedic Goddess stands for the same divine Power that in later times came to be venerated as Shakti and evoked as the serpent power.

What the various models describing the evolution of sound or vibration have in common is the idea that there are at least three levels at which sound exists. The Tantric scriptures distinguish between:

1. *pashyantî-vâc* ("visible speech")—the most subtle form

of sound visible only to intuition;

2. *madhyamâ-vâc* ("intermediate speech")—sound at the subtle level of existence, which is the voice of thought;

3. *vaikharî-vâc* ("manifest speech")—audible sound transmitted through vibration of the air.

Beyond these three is the transcendental level called *parâ-vâc* or "supreme speech," which is Shakti in perfect union with Shiva. It is soundless sound, hinted at in the *Rig-Veda* (10.129) in the phrase "the One breathed breathlessly."

The three levels of sound correspond to the three forms or levels of the serpent power:

1. *ûrdhva-kundalinî* ("upper serpent"), which is the *kundalinî* primarily active in the *âjnâ-cakra* and tending to ascend toward the thousand-petaled lotus at the crown of the head;[6]

2. *madhya-kundalinî* ("middle serpent"), which is the Goddess power active in the region of the heart and capable of ascending or descending;

3. *adhah-kundalinî* ("lower serpent"), which is the psycho-spiritual energy primarily associated with the three lower *cakras*.

In its divine aspect, the serpent power is known as *parâ-kundalinî*, or Shakti per se. From the perspective of Tantric philosophy, every single form or aspect of the universe is a manifestation of that ultimate Power and a symbol for it. In light of contemporary quantum physics, the "energy language" of Tantra makes more sense than perhaps it did to outsiders at the time of its creation two thousand and more years ago.

In its upward passage through the body's axial pathway, the Goddess power step by step dissolves the *cakras*.

This can also be understood in sonic terms. According to almost identical descriptions found in various *Tantras*, when the *kundalinî* leaves the bottom *cakra*, it gathers in the fundamental energies captured in the four letters inscribed in the four petals of the *mûlâdhâra* lotus. It then proceeds to the second *cakra* where it gathers the six letter-energies from there, and so on. Finally, the letter energies of the *âjnâ-cakra* are dissolved into the transcendental seed-point together with the *cakra* itself. When all fifty letters of the alphabet, or basic vibrations, are thus dissolved, enlightenment occurs. The *Shâradâ-Tilaka-Tantra* (5.121-132) describes a form of initiation (*dîkshâ*) in which the teacher enters the disciple's body and performs this process himself. This is also known as *vedha-dîkshâ* or "initiation by penetration."

The Nature of Mantras

The fifty letters (*varna*) of the Sanskrit alphabet, which in a way represent the body of the *kundalinî*, are called "matrices" (*mâtrikâ*)—a term that can also mean "little mothers." They are the wombs of all sounds that make up language and are embedded in the subtle sound (*nâda*). These letters produce not only secular words but also the sacred sounds called *mantras*. A *mantra* can consist of a single letter, a syllable, a word, or even an entire phrase. Thus the vowel *a*, the syllable *âh*, the word *aham* ("I"), or the phrase *shivo'ham* ("I am Shiva," consisting of *shivah* and *aham*) can serve in a mantric capacity. In addition, the four Vedic hymnodies (*Rig-Veda, Yajur-Veda, Sâma-Veda,* and *Atharva-Veda*) have traditionally been held to consist of *mantras* only, because the hymns have all been revealed by seers (*rishi*).

The word *mantra* is composed of the verbal root *man* ("to think") and the suffix *tra* (indicating instrumentality). Thus a *mantra* is literally an instrument of thought.

In his *Vimarshinî* commentary on the *Shiva-Sûtra* (1.1.), Kshemarâja explains that a *mantra* is "that by which one secretly considers or inwardly reflects on one's identity with the nature of the supreme Lord." This interpretation focuses on the connection between *mantra* and *manana* ("thinking, considering, reflecting"). According to another traditional etymology, *mantra* gets its name from providing protection (*trâna*) for the mind (*manas*).

Far from being nonsense syllables, as an earlier generation of scholars has claimed, *mantras* are creative forces that act directly upon consciousness. But for a sound to have mantric potency it must have been transmitted by an initiate. In other words, the famous *om*-sound on its own is no more a *mantra* than the word "dog." It acquires mantric value only when it has been empowered by an adept and transmitted to a disciple. This is a vitally important point that is generally unknown to Western seekers. The reason why *mantras* can be thus potentized at all is that they have the Goddess power for their essence. "Without Her," declares the *Tantra-Sadbhâva*, "they are as unproductive as clouds in autumn."[7] But only an adept in whom the *kundalinî* is awake can empower a sound—*any* sound—so that it is transmuted into a *mantra*. As Shiva tells his divine spouse in the *Mahânirvâna-Tantra* (5.18a), "O Beloved, your *mantras* are countless."

Successful *mantra* practice not only depends on proper initiation but also on realizing the essence behind the sound. This is made clear in the *Shrî-Kanthîya-Samhitâ* (as quoted in the *Vimarshinî* 2.1.), which states:

> So long as the *mantrin* is distinct from the *mantra*, he cannot be successful. Wisdom alone must be the root of all this; otherwise he is not successful.

A *mantra* must be awakened (*prabuddha*) in order to unleash its inherent power. This is also known as "mantric consciousness" (*mantra-caitanya*), which goes beyond the audible sound to the level of psychospiritual power itself. As the Western adept Swami Chetanananda explains:

> Ultimately, our practice of any mantra is intended to refine our awareness to the point where we experience that pulsation going on within us all the time. When we can do that, we forget about the mantra itself because we are now aware, instead, of the dynamic event going on within and around us. As a result, the total vibration of what we are is changed. In the process, we transform ourselves.[8]

A *mantra* lacking in "consciousness" is just like any other sound. As the *Kulárnava-Tantra* (15.61-64) states:

> *Mantras* without consciousness are said to be mere letters. They yield no result even after a trillion recitations.
>
> The state that manifests promptly when the *mantra* is recited [with "consciousness"], that result is not [to be gained] from a hundred, a thousand, a hundred thousand, or ten million recitations.
>
> Kuleshvarî, the knots at the heart and throat are pierced, all the limbs are invigorated, tears of joy, goose-flesh, bodily ecstasy, and tremulous speech suddenly occur for sure...
>
> ...when a *mantra* endowed with consciousness is uttered even once. Where such signs are seen, the [*mantra*] is said to be according to tradition.

In order to charge up, "strengthen," a *mantra* one should repeat it thousands of times—a technique called *purashcarana* ("preliminary practice"). As the *Shrî-Tattva-Cintâmani* (20.3-4) states:

> Just as the body is incapable of action without the

psyche, so also is said to be a *mantra* without the preliminary practice.

Therefore the foremost of practitioners should first undertake the preliminary practice. Only through such application can the deity [of a *mantra*] be brought under control.

The last stanza contains an explanation for the difference between a *mantra* and an ordinary sound. While all sounds are ultimately manifestations of the divine Power, *mantras* as it were are especially concentrated expressions of Shakti. This gives them their particular potency and usefulness on the spiritual path. The idea of bringing a deity under control may sound strange or even offensive to Western ears, but according to Tantra these deities (*devatâ*) are in the final analysis simply higher types of psycho-spiritual energy. Because they are intelligent forces and appear to have a personal center, the Tantric practitioners are mindful to relate to them with appropriate respect and devotion. They understand, however, that these deity-energies are their own true nature, the Self. To bring a deity under control means to be able to use his or her specific energy for the spiritual process or even for worldly ends. The Tantric practitioners must constantly juggle the twofold recognition that there is only the One and that this Singularity (*ekatva*) appears differentiated at the level of phenomenal existence. Thus they know that they are both devotee and the ultimate object of devotion.

The *Mantra-Yoga-Samhitâ* contains detailed information about selecting a *mantra* for a disciple, auspicious and inauspicious days for imparting a *mantra*, and the various fruits of mantric practice. *Mantras* can be employed both for liberation and other secondary purposes, such as combating illness or evil influences, or gaining wealth and power. Most high-minded practitioners are reluctant to use *mantras* for anything other than the greatest human goal (*purusha-artha,* written *purushârtha*), which is liberation. In Tantric rituals, *mantras* are used to purify the altar, one's seat, implements such as vessels and offering spoons, or the offerings themselves (e.g., flowers, water, food), or to invoke deities and protectors, and so on. Yet, the science of sacred sound (*mantra-shâstra*) has since ancient times been widely put to secular use as well. In this case, *mantras* assume the character of magical spells rather than sacred vibrations in the service of self-transformation and self-transcendence.

The *Kulaarnava-Tantra* (15.65-70) mentions sixty defects that can render *mantra* practice futile. To list only some of these: A *mantra* can be "blocked" (by duplicating a syllable), "wrongly syllabled," "broken," "lifeless," "defiled," "unstable," "fear-instilling," "powerless," and "deluded." In order to remedy these shortcomings, the *Shâradâ-Tilaka-Tantra* (2.111) recommends the practice of *yoni-mudrâ*.[10] This technique, which is well known from Hatha-Yoga scriptures, is performed by contracting the muscles of the perineum, which causes the vital energy to rise. In addition, however, the Tantric practitioner should visualize the fifty letters of the alphabet ascending from the psycho-spiritual center at the base of the spine to the *cakra* at the crown of the head. This text (2.112ff.) also gives an alternative to this practice, which can be found in the *Kula-Arnava-Tantra* (15.71-72) as well. These are the following ten remedial practices (*samskâra*):

1. Creating (*janana*)—extracting a *mantra's* constituent syllables from the alphabet;

2. enlivening (*jîvana*)—reciting each syllable separately with the *om*-sound prefixed to it;

3. hammering (*tâdana*)—sprinkling each written syl-

lable of a *mantra* with water while reciting the seed syllable yam (for the air element);

4. awakening (*bodhana*)—touching each written syllable with a red oleander flower while reciting the seed syllable *ram* (for the fire element); the number of flowers should correspond to the number of syllables;

5. consecrating (*abhisheka*)—sprinkling each written syllable with water containing the twigs of the *ashvattha* tree (the sacred fig tree); the number of twigs should correspond to the number of syllables;

6. cleansing (*vimalî-karana*)—visualizing a *mantra's* impurities being burned by reciting *om hraum,* which is the *mantra* for light;

7. strengthening (*âpyâyana*)—sprinkling each written syllable with water containing *kusha* grass;

8. offering water (*tarpana*)—offering water to the *mantra* while saying, "I satiate *mantra* so-and-so";

9. offering light (*dîpana*)—prefixing the seed syllables *om hrîm shrîm* to a *mantra*;

10. concealing (*gupti*)—keeping one's *mantra* secret.

Mantras of concentrated potency are known as "seed syllables" (*bîja*). *Om* is the original seed syllable, the source of all others. The *Mantra-Yoga-Samhitâ* (71) calls it the "best of all *mantras*," adding that all other *mantras* receive their power from it. Thus *om* is prefixed or suffixed to numerous *mantras*:

Om namah shivâya. "Om. Obeisance to Shiva."

Om namo bhagavate. "Om. Obeisance to the Lord [Krishna or Vishnu]."

Om namo ganeshâya. "Om. Obeisance to [the elephant-

Om namo nârâyanâya. "*Om.* Obeisance to Narayana [Vishnu]."

Om bhûr bhuvah svah tat savitur varenyam bhargo devasya dhîmahi dhiyo yo nah pracodayât. "*Om.* Earth. Midregion. Heaven. Let us contemplate the most excellent splendor of Savitri, so that He may inspire our visions." (This is the famous Vedic *gâyatrî-mantra*.)

Om shânte prashânte sarva-krodha-upashamani svâhâ. "*Om.* At peace! Pacifying! All anger be subdued! Hail!" (Note pronunciation: *sarva-krodhopashamani*)

Om sac-cid-ekam brahma. "*Om.* The singular Being-Consciousness, the Absolute."

The *Mahânirvâna-Tantra* (3.13) calls the last-mentioned *brahma-mantra* the most excellent of all *mantras*, which promptly bestows not only liberation but also virtue, wealth, and pleasure. It is suitable for all practitioners and does not require careful computations before it is given. "Merely by receiving the *mantra*," this scripture (3.24) claims, "the person is filled with the Absolute." And, this *Tantra* (3.26) continues, "guarded by the *brahma-mantra* and surrounded with the splendor of the Absolute, he becomes radiant like another sun for all the planets etc."

Over many centuries, the Vedic and Tantric masters have conceived, or rather envisioned, numerous other primary power sounds besides *om*. These seed-syllables (*bîja*), as they are called, can be used on their own or, more commonly, in conjunction with other power sounds forming a mantric phrase. According to the *Mantra-Yoga-Samhitâ* (71), there are eight primary *bîja-mantras*, which are helpful in all kinds of circumstances but which yield their deeper mystery only to the *yogin*:

1. *aim* (pronounced "I'm")—*guru-bîja* ("seed-syllable of the teacher"), also called *vahni-jâyâ* ("Agni's wife");
2. *hrîm*—*shakti-bîja* ("seed-syllable of Shakti"), also called *mâyâ-bîja*;
3. *klîm*—*kâma-bîja* ("seed-syllable of desire");
4. *krîm*—*yoga-bîja* ("seed-syllable of union"), also called *kâli-bîja*;
5. *shrîm*—*ramâ-bîja* ("seed-syllable of delight"); Ramâ is another name for Lakshmî, the Goddess of Fortune; hence this seed-syllable is also known as *lakshmî-bîja*;
6. *trîm*—*teja-bîja* ("seed-syllable of fire");
7. *strîm*—*shânti-bîja* ("seed-syllable of peace");
8. *hlîm*—*rakshâ-bîja* ("seed-syllable of protection");

Other schools or texts furnish different names for these eight primary *bîjas* or even altogether different schemas. Some other well-known seed-syllables are *lam, vam, ram, yam, ham* (all associated with the five elements and the lower five *cakras*), *hum, hûm* (called *varman* or "shield"), and *phat* (called *astra* or "weapon").

The Art of Recitation

When a practitioner has received a *mantra* from the mouth of an initiate, he or she can be confident of success in mantric recitation (*japa*), providing of course all the instructions for proper recitation are followed as well. Mindfulness, regularity, and a large number of repetitions of the *mantra* are the three most important requirements. Also, there are certain sacred places where *mantra* practice is considered very auspicious. According to the *Kula-*

Arnava-Tantra (15.25), *japa* near one's teacher, a *brahmin*, a cow, a tree, water, or a sacred fire is particularly promising. This text (15.46-47) additionally prescribes the practice of "infusion" (*nyâsa*) for mantric recitation.

Japa can be performed in three fundamental ways: verbalized (*vâcika*), whispered (*upâmshu*), and mentally (*mânasa*). The first style is audible recitation and is considered inferior to the other two styles. In whispered recitation only the lips move but no audible sound escapes them. Superior to this style is mental recitation where attention is fixed exclusively on the inner meaning of the *mantra*.

Twenty-one, 108, or 1008 repetitions are considered auspicious. But for the *mantra* to unlock its potency (*vîrya*), hundreds of thousands of repetitions may be necessary. Once this has occurred, however, even a single pronunciation of the *mantra* will make its power available to the *mantrin* or *japin*, the reciter of *mantras*. In practice, after a while, the *mantra* recites itself spontaneously, and its intrinsic power can be felt as a steady charge of energy present in one's body. This is *ajapa-japa,* or "unrecited recitation"—also known as the *hamsa-mantra*—which is more than the mental "echo" that occurs when we repeat a word over and over again. It is not simply a mental groove caused by verbal repetition but a mind-transforming energetic state of being.

It is important to keep a record of the number of repetitions. This is generally done by means of a rosary (*mâlâ*). Rosaries may consist of 15, 24, 27, 30, 50 or, most commonly, 108 beads (plus one "master bead," representing one's *guru* or Mount Meru, a symbol for the central channel). The numeral 108 has been held sacred and auspicious in India since ancient times. Various interpretations have been offered for this highly symbolic number, but the most likely explanation lies in astronomy.

Already in the Vedic era, the sages were aware of the fact that the moon's and also the sun's average distance from the earth is 108 times their respective diameters. As the American Vedic researcher Subhash Kak has shown, this number was crucial in the construction of the Vedic fire altar.[11] Symbolically speaking, 108 is the number signifying the mid-region (*antariksha*), the space between heaven and earth. Thus the 108 beads can be taken to represent an equal number of steps from the material world to the luminous realm of the divine Reality-India's version of Jacob's ladder.

The rosary is often referred to as *aksha-mâlâ*, which corresponds to the *varna-mâlâ* or "garland of letters" of the Sanskrit language. The Sanskrit word *aksha* means "eye," but in the present context refers to the letters *a* and *ksha*, the Sanskrit equivalents of the Greek *alpha* and *omega*. Thus the rosary (of fifty beads) represents the entire alphabet. The *Kulaarnava-Tantra* (15.48) distinguishes between an actual and an imaginary rosary. The former is composed of the fifty letters of the Sanskrit alphabet. The beads of the latter can be made from sandal wood, crystal, shell, coral, or most commonly *rudra-aksha* ("Rudra's eye," written *rudrâksha*), which is the multifaced seed of the blue marble tree sacred to Shiva. The *Mantra-Yoga-Samhitâ* (76) mentions all kinds of other materials that can profitably be used to make a rosary. Like any ritual object, the rosary too must be purified before use. The *Mahânirvâna-Tantra* (6.171b-172a) furnishes the following mantric utterance for this purpose:

> O rosary! O rosary! O great calculator! You are the essence of all power.
>
> In You are found the four goals [i.e., material prosperity, pleasure, morality, and liberation]. Therefore grant me all success.

Another traditional way of keeping track of the number of repetitions is by counting with one's fingers. Various methods are known and some are specific to certain *mantras*. It is considered inauspicious to count merely with the tip of one's fingers, and instead one should, according to the *Mantra-Yoga-Samhitâ* (75), count using all the phalanxes.

A *mantra* should be recited with the right intonation, as learned from one's teacher, and also at the proper pace. If, as the *Kulárnava-Tantra* (15.55) makes clear, it is repeated too fast, there is the danger of disease. If it is recited too slowly, however, it will diminish one's energy. In either case, japa will be "useless like water in a broken vessel." This *Tantra* (15.57-58), furthermore, points out the natural impurities at the onset and the closing of recitation, which must be countermanded by a special mantric practice, namely by reciting the mantra seven or 108 times with *om* at the beginning and the end.

Because *mantras* must be recited numerous times over many hours every day before they can bear fruit, it is easy for a practitioner to get tired. In that case the scriptures typically recommend shifting from *japa* to meditation. Then again, when the mind is exhausted from meditation, switching back to reciting one's *mantra* can bring renewed vigor and enthusiasm.

Mantras may not only be spoken or mentally recited but can also be written out on paper, metal, cloth, or other materials. This technique is known as *likhita-japa*, which, in the words of Swami Sivananda Radha, "brings peace, poise and strength within."[12] The same is of course true of other forms of *japa* as well. As with all yogic or practices, the success of *mantra* recitation depends to a large degree on the practitioner's motivation and dedication.

Foot Notes

1. J. Woodroffe, *The Garland of Letters: Studies in the Mantra-Shastra* (Madras: Ganesh & Company, 6th ed. 1974), p. 230.

2. G. Krishna, *Kundalini: The Evolutionary Energy in Man* (London: Robinson & Watkins, 1971), p. 88.

3. The word *vânî* suggests speech that is musical and beautiful.

4. The Tantras distinguish between a Vedic, Shaiva, and Shâkta *pranava*. The first-mentioned is the *Om*-sound, the second is *hum*, and the third is *hrîm*.

5. Other subtle distinctions are known as well. See G. Feuerstein, "The Sacred Syllable Om," *Yoga Research and Education Center Studies Series,* no. 2 (Lower Lake, Calif.: Yoga Research and Education Center, 1997).

6. The terms *ûrdhva-* and *adhah-kundalinî* are also used to refer to the ascending and descending movement of the serpent power respectively.

7. In Northern India, the autumnal skies are brilliant and largely free from clouds. When a cloud does appear, it will not produce rain.

8. The *mantrin* is a practitioner reciting a *mantra*.

9. Swami Chetanananda, *Dynamic Stillness* (Cambridge, Mass.: Rudra Press, 1990), p. 145.

10. Some Tantric texts explain *yoni-mudrâ* differently in the present context.

11. See S. Kak, "The Astronomy of the Vedic Altars and the Rgveda," *The Mankind Quarterly,* vol. 33, no. 1 (1992), pp. 43-55.

12. Swami Sivanananda Radha, *Mantras: Words of Power* (Porthill, Id.: Timeless Books, 1980), p. 8.

1

THE MANTRA WHICH IS IRRESISTIBLE IN THE THREE WORLDS

The God said:-

Now I shall narrate the Mantra which is irresistible in the three worlds (Trailokhya Vijaya) and which tramples down the spell of all other incantations. The Mantra is as follows:—Om, Hum, Kshoun, Hrum, Om, obeisance to the fierce-mouthed, horrid-jawed goddess. Dost thou sport amorously, O thou possessed of terrible features. Let thy diabolical laughter reverberate the atmosphere, O thou goddess with blood-shot eyes, shriek and sound, O thou, goddess of infernal sound, and who art possessed of lightning tongues. Be manifest, O thou goddess, of extremely emaciated features. Put on thy mantle, O thou clad in the coils of the serpent known as the Gonasha. Drive every thing before thee, oh thou who wearest a garland of dead human bodies. Yawn and open thy fierce mouth, oh thou goddess who art clad in raw hydes. Dance and dance with thy sword flashing forth lightning in all directions, with thy face made doubly fierce by sullen look and thy eyebrows arched in rage. Roar and roar, oh thou besmeared with the smelling fetid fat of dead bodies thou art fond of. Laugh and laugh, get furious and furious, oh goddess, shine forth in terrible splendour, oh thou coloured like the blue lightning and decorated with garlands of black cloud. Attract and draw forth the minds of men, oh thou dawn-complexioned goddess bestriding a lion, and who art bedecked with bells and Ravavas. Om Ham Hrim Hrun, thou fierce looking goddess, Hun, Hring, Kling, Om Hrum, Hum, Attract. Om shake and shake, Om Ha, Has Khas. O thou thunder wielding goddess, Hum, Kshum, Ksham, oh thou who art manifest as anger. Burn and burn, Om, oh thou the most terrible of all terrors, and break and break (the ranks of my enemy's forces,) cut and cut them through, oh thou goddess of immense proportions. Om, oh thou fierce-jawed mother of all ghosts and goblins, and destructress of all evils, I make salutation unto thee. Oh thou ever victorious and ever irresistible in the three worlds. Hrim Fut obeisance to thee. The goddess should be propitiated in connection with an act of victory or with any act undertaken to ensure victory in war, and should be meditated upon as possessed of a blue complexion and twenty hands and as standing on the dead bodies of men. The rite of Nayasa should be performed over the five different parts of the body as herebefore enjoined, and oblations composed of red flowers and clarified butter should be offered in the consecrated fire. A mere repitition of the abovesaid Mantra which is known as the conqueror of the three worlds (Trailokya Vijaya) will put the hostile forces to utter rout. (1-2)

"Om obeisance to the god revealed in a variety of shapes (Vahurupa). Stupefy and stupefy, and make spellbound the faculties of (my enemies,) and scatter and scattar them to the four quarters of the globe. Om charm the God Brahma, charm the God Vishnu, and Om charm the God Maheshvara (Siva). Make the god Indra tremble in his throne. Uproot the mountains of the earth, dry up the seven oceans Om, cut through and cut through the forces sent against me. I make salutation unto the god Vahurupa." At the time of repeating the above incantation, the votary should contemplate the moulded serpent on the body of clay image of the god as representing his enemy.

11

THE INCANTATION FOR OBTAINING VICTORIES IN THE THREE WORLDS

THE GOD SAID:-

Now I shall narrate to you the incantation which should be read for obtaining victories in war and which is accordingly named as the Sangram Vijaya Vidya (victory winning incantation). The Mantra is as follows:—"Om Hrim, oh thou Goddess Chamunda, who dwellest in the cremation ground (of the Universe) and who wieldest a Khattanga and a human skull in thy two hands and standest on the body of (the primordial matter of universal dissolution represented by the god Maheshvara) or the Mahashava (the supreme dead), surrounded by the extremely attenuated ether pervading the dying space in a disintegrating universe, (Mahavimana). Obstruct the apertures of the globe with thy indomitable powers, do that, do that, oh thou symbol of the primal night who art surrounded by the might Ganas (a class of demigods), manifest thy all obstructing prowess, O thou immense-mouthed goddess bedecked with little drums, bells and kinkinis and whose laughter shakes the worlds in their orbits. Om, Hrum, Fut, (salutation with a view to obtain thy tutelary protection.) Advance and advance, O thou goddess, whose jagged teeth casts down the gloom of night and who art clad in an elephant-skin. Advance and advance, O Goddess, with an extremely haggard and emaciated frame, and whose footsteps are followed by a concourse of many unearthly sounds, advance and advance, oh thou the supreme absolute monstress with a complexion like the flashes of heaven, advance and advance with thy horrid teeth exposed in a demoniac laughter and thy bloody tongues protuding out of thy terrible mouth devouring fresh victims. Om Chili, Chili, oh thou goddess with a pair of beautiful eyes agile as the bird called the Chakora (a fabulous bird of extreme agility supposed to live upon the ambrosia shed down by the full moon) Om, obstruct the apertures of the universe with thy mighty prowess, Oh thou goddess with an ever protruding tongue, manifest thy prowess. Om Bhim, Oh thou goddess whose sullen look inspires terror in the breasts of all beings (Bhrukuti Mākhi), and whose roar and battle-cry strikes terror into the breasts of all who hear them. Show thy mettle, Oh goddess, on the crest of whose crown shines the moon occasionally obstructed by the clotted hairs dangling loosely from its (crown) inside. Make thy weird laughter resound the welkin in one unbroken and continuous echo. Om Hrum, accomplish such and such an end of mine (the votary should here state the particular object he has in view for repeating this incantation). Accomplish and accomplish this end of mine, Oh goddess, whose mouth vomits forth primal darkness through the interestices of thy horrible teeth, and who art the protrectress from all banes and evils that beset our mundane existence. Soon and very soon accomplish this end.

Om Fut to thee. Om subjugate with thy mace all the forces of my enemy, cut through and cut through their ranks, Oh goddess.

Om, dance and dance and sport in death, shake and shake my enemies and turn them topsyturvy.

Kill and kill, Oh thou goddess who dost fondly relish human flesh and blood, trample down and trample down, Om, pierce through and pierce through, Om slay and slay, Om chase and pursue, Om fell to the ground the enemy though bearing a charmed life and possessed of a body hard as the bolt of heaven. Om, stupefy and cut once and for all the evil doors dwelling in the three worlds whether captured or at large. Dance and dance in the battle array, Oh thou goddess with eyes sunk in their sockets and a face resembling that of an owl, and a head rendered doubly ghastly by hairs standing erect on their roots. Burn and burn the enemy's forces, Oh thou goddess wearing a human skull in thy hand, and bedecked with a similar garland. Om, cook, and cook the armed hosts sent against me, and enter the ranks of [my] enemy's troops arranged in battle array. Om, why dost thou tarry goddess, overwhelm them all with the might of the gods Brahma, Vishnu, Rudra, and that born of the essence of the sainted beings (Rishis).

Om, obstruct and impede the progress of the marching hosts, and break and break their arms and weapons, Oh thou terrible looking goddess, with black serpents coiling round thy body. Break and Break their ranks, Oh thou who dost confound all order among the troops drawn up in circles and squares, and make all sorts of manoeuveres impossible, and from whose nostrils hang down snakes reaching down thy protruded lips rendered doubly dreadful by thy ferocious mouth scantly hid by thy dark brown clotted hairs. Yell and yell, Oh thou goddess, whose mouth vomits forth fatal fire, undermine, tumble down, and uplift the ground they stand upon.

Om, make my head cool, Oh goddess, let my hand and feet resume their former wonted activity and vigour. Let my eyes be opened and let my bodily organs work in their natural health, Om Fut.

Om, cut and pierce through with thy trident, kill with thy thunder, strike with thy club, cleave with thy quoit, Om, pierce with thy spear, bite with thy teeth, fell with thy Karnika, attack with thy mace the fever which follows a distinct periodicity and occur on the every second, third, (tertian) or the fourth day from its first paroxysm. Set at naught the influences of the malignant spirits such as the Dakinis and the Skan as and those of the baneful planets. Exorcise them all and take thy seat on the spirits, formerly possessed by them. Come, Oh thou wife of Brahma who art also revealed as the wives of Kumar and Maheshwar. Come, come, Oh Vaishnavi, come, Oh Bhairabi, come, Oh Aindri, come, Oh Chamunde. Om, come, Oh Revati, come, Oh thou Revati of the skies, come, Oh thou goddess who dwellest on the summits of the Himalaya. Come, Oh thou goddess, who hast slain the demon Ruru and annihilated the whole race of demons. Come, Oh thou goddess, whose thoroughfare is the heaven itself, cast thy noose and pierce with thy mace. Stop and enter (the line of the hostile armies) parlyse their sense organs such as the mouths, hands and feet, cast a stupefying influence in all directions, charm the cardinal and angular points of the skies and all spaces whether above or below this terrestrial globe. Om, stupefy all, either through ashes, drinking water or through the subsoil. Om, fell them, Om obeisance to Chamunda Kili, Kili Om, Vichale, Hum, Fut.

The incantation laid down above should be deemed as a potent factor in bringing about the fulfilment of all ends and desires, and which being read after the performance of the necessary Homa and the Japa (repetition of a Mantra) ceremony enables a man to win a battle. The presiding goddess of the incantation should be meditated upon as possessed of twenty-eight hands, weilding in them, a sword, a khetaka, a club, a mace, a bow, an arrow, a clenched fist, a club, a conch shell, a sword, a banner, a thunder-bolt, a quoit, a battle-axe, a hand-drum, a mirror, a spear, tuft of hair, a phoughshare, a Mushala, a noose, a Tomara, a drum, a Panara, a blessing and a fist respectively. The goddess should be contemplated as standing on a buffalo in the attitude of slaying that engaged animal. The Homa spoken of above should be performed with a composition consisting of honey, sugar, and clarified butter. This incantation should not be disclosed to every body (I-6).

III

THE SIX SORTS OF CHARMS

THE GOD SAID:—

Now I shall describe the six sorts of charms which are usually known as the SHATKARMA (such as the acts of killing, stupefying, etc., by means of incantations). The Mantras which should be used in connection herewith are as follows:—First the Sadhya Mantras should be laid down followed by the (principal) one. The Mantra thus combined and formed is known as the Pallava, and should be used in connection with all acts undertaken with a view to district the minds of one's enemies. The Mantras known as the Yogakshya consists of the principal Mantra, being written or mentioned at the beginning, followed by the Sadhya one, which in its turn, should be followed by the principal Mantra. The foregoing Mantra should be used on occasions where the votary would wish for the extirpation of the whole race of his enemy. The Mantra known as the Rodhaka and which consists of the Mantra being written first, succeeded by the Sadhya Mantra, respectively followed in their turn by the principal and the Sadhya Mantras, should be made use of in all acts undertaken with the sole object of stupefying the faculties of one's enemies. The Mantras which are denominated as the Samputas, consists in the Sadhyamantras being written at the middle and above and below the principal one on its left hand side and should be used in attracting and gaining a control over another's mind (1-5).

When the letters composing any particular Mantra fall under the category of Sadhya letters, the Mantra passes by the denomination of the class first stated above (Prathama), and is to be employed in acts, undertaken with a view to gain an ascendancy or control over another's mind. The Vidarvha class of Mantras consists in the two of the letters constituting the Mantra being written at the beginning followed by a Sadhya letter and is to be made use of in incantations producing similar results as the above. (6-7).

The incantations in connection with the acts of attracting or charming the mind of another person should be performed in the spring time (Vasanta), as well as incantations for subduing high fever, and the term "Svaha" should be used therein on all occasions where a term signifying obeisance would be necessary. The term "Namaskar" (obeisance) should be used in all charms practised with a view to confer peace and prosperity on a particular individual, while the term "Vasat" should be employed in incantations which would have the enjoyment or restoration of good health as their object. In all deadly incantations, as well as in those practised with a view to create a dissension between a previously attached couple or practised with the object of distracting the mind of one's adversary, the term "Fut" should be used on occasions requiring a term of salutation. The term "Vasat" should be held as specially auspicious for all acts connected with the spiritual initiation of a person, and should be also used in the rites which give the votaries success in enterprize and accession of wealth in general (8-10).

The votary should close a deadly incantation by repeating the following verse. "Thou art, Oh Yama, the god of death, who holdest sway over the region of the departed. This ceaseless, infinite time is thy embodiment, and thou dealest with the departed souls according to their deserts. I offer this enemy to thee, as a victim. Kill him without delay." Then the priest officiating at the ceremony and who should be looked upon as the destroyer of al people antagonistic to the votary, should address him in a pleasant vein as follows: "Hold, Hold, Oh votary. Rest assured I shall spare no pain to kill and overwhelm him with ruin." Then the god of death should be worshipped and propitiated with white lotus flowers and the votary should deem himself indentical with the god Bhairava and contemplate the goddess Kuleshvari in his heart. Then a Homa ceremony should be performed in honour of the presiding deity of death, whereby the object of the undertaking would be fulfilled. In the night, the votary would learn in sleep the result of the incantation both as regards himself and his adversary. A man, by worshipping the goddess Durga with the Mantra running as 'Salutation to thee, O Durga O Durga who art the protectress of the universe," would be able to destroy his enemies, whereas a continuous repetition of, "Ha, Sa, Ksha, Ma, La, Va, Ra, and Ya, Mantra," sacred to the goddess Bhairavi, would be attended by the same result (11-14).

IV

THE MEDICINAL OR CURATIVE INCANTATIONS

THE GOD SAID:—

Now I shall speak about the medicinal or curative incantations which grant all wished for objects to individuals (I). The number of the letters composing the name of a thief should be doubled and added with the number of its Matras multiplied by four. The total thus obtained should be divided by the number of letters constituting the name of a person who should be reckoned as a thief in the event of there being left any remainder (2).

Now I shall dwell upon the process of reckoning the birth of a male or a female child in the womb. If the question put to the soothsayer consists of an odd number of letters, the child in the womb should be reckoned as belonging to the male sex. The child would be born blind, and the defect would be in the left eye in the event of the component letters of the name (sic) being of an even number, while the defect would be in the right eye in case where the letters would number otherwise. The number of letters composing the names of both the man and the wife should be multiplied with the number of their Matras and divided by four. The quotient, if even, would indicate the birth of a male child, while an odd quotient obtained in the aforesaid way would indicate the birth of a female child. Any remainder being left in the later case would predict the death of the wife before that of her husband, while the one remaining in the former instance would foretell the survival of the wife (3-5).

Now I shall describe the Shani Chakra, or the diagram by which the malignant influence of the Saturn lying in the particular quarters of the globe on a particular day may be ascertained. The Saturn occupying the particular sign of a month caste a full glance at the second, seventh, eighth and the tenth part of a day marked by the same and a half glance at its fourth and the eleventh part. A malignant glance of the Saturn should be carefully avoided. The presiding planet of a day (Dinadhipa) casts its peculiar influence for three hours only while the rest of the planets exert similar influences for half a Yama (eighth part of a day) respectively. The part of the day assigned to the Saturn, should be avoided in war (6-

7).

Now I shall describe the position of the Rahu as it varies from day to day in a week. The Rahu lies at the east on a Sunday, at the north-west on a Saturday, at the south on a Thursday, at the south-east on a Friday and a Tuesday, and at the north on a Wednesday, while at the same time the Phani Rahu lies enclosing the south-west, south-east, and north-west quarters of the glob for three hours only. A man who starts on a journey to a direction occupied by the Rahu, meets his doom, though powerful as Indra (the lord of the gods) himself (8).

Now I shall describe the position of the Rahu on the different days of a lunar month (Tithi). The Rahu lies in the south-east and the north-west on the days of a full and a new moon respectively. The Rahu is sure to kill one's enemy journeying towards his face. The Rahu lies in the front of the Tithis of which the letters Ka to Ja are the symbols, and in the east on the Tithis of which the letters Dha to Ma stand for, and accordingly the groups of Mars should be avoided in a light fortnight.

Now I shall describe the Visti Rahu. Eight straight lines should be laid down and the progress of the Rahu should be ascertained as follows:—From the north-east the Visti Rahu goes over to the south, from the sough, to the north-west, from the north-west to the east, from the east by the south-west to the north, form the north to the south-east, and thence by the west to the north-east. The mighty Rahu travels with the Visti as stated above, and occupies the north-east quarter of the sky on the third day of a lunar month, and the southern on its seventh day.

thus in the light and the dark fortnights the Rahu kills one's enemies situate at the quarter from which the wind blows.

Now I shall describe the incantation by which the body of a person may be made hard and proof against all blows and weapons (Dridhi Karanam). The charm should be put in an amulet and worn at the neck or on the arm. The stems of Kandulakshya culled under the influence of the asterism Pushya and a recitation of the Aparajita Mantra would make a sword inert. The Mantra is as follows:- "Om obeisance to the goddess Vajrashrinkhala, kill and kill, Om, eat and eat, devour and devour. Om, drink the blood of my enemy out of thy cup of a human skull. Om obstruct and obstruct the eastern quarter of the sky, O thou goddess with bloodshot eyes, besmeared with ashes, clad in bloody clothes, and equipped with the bolt of thunder. Om, close up, and close up the western gate of the sky. Om, close up and close up the southern quarter of the globe. Om, barricade the northern entrance of the sky. Om, hold in check the Nagas (the serpent spirits). Om, keep in custody their wives. Om, keep in control the demon world. Om, put under curb and rein the fiendish activity of the infernal beings such as the Yakshas, Rakshasas and the Pishachas. Om bind and bind in an unbreakable chord. Om, Protect and protect me from all evils which are engendered by the evil spirits, ghosts, and Gandharvas. Om, protect and keep secure (for me) the space upward. Keep secure and guard the space downward. Om, bind the Kshorika. Om, burn and burn. O thou goddess of mighty prowess. Om Ghoti, Ghoti, Mothi, Mothi to thee, O thou goddess, who art encircled by a wall of liquid thunder dripping down from thy dishevelled hairs. Hun Fut, Hrun, Hrun, Shrun, Fut to thee. Hrun, Has, Fan, Fen Fus, protect and protect me from all malignant stars and planets. Protect me from (the influences of) all diseases, keep me secure from the infinite harms and evils that beset human life. The above incantation should be used in all sorts of fever and specially in cases where possessions by evil spirits are suspected, as well as in acts any way connected with any sort of spell or charm (9-20).

V

TRIKHANDI MANTRAS

THE GOD SAID:—

Now I shall enumerate the Trikhandi Mantras which are as follows:—"Om, obeisance to the god Rudra, obeisance to Chamunda, obeisance to the Akashamatris. Blessed are the epithets of the Akasha Matris who are immortal and are free from all decay and afflictions which our mortal frames are heir to, and whose unobstructed way lies throughout the universe. Yea, blessed are the Mantras presided over by the Akasha Matrikas who incessantly change their own shapes and assume any shape they please, and who can subjugate, charm, banish and destroy any creature they like. The following is the most mysterious and most secret of the Mantras sacred to the Matris whereby the highest salvation is attained, other men's incantations are nullified, and the greatest success is achieved. In the Brahmakhandapada, or the part presided over by the god Brahma, the following hundred and twenty-one padas or terms have been held sacred to the goddess:- "Om obeisance (Svaha) to the goddess Chamunda who is the wife of the god Brahma and who grants all boons (Varada), is devoid of all illusion and crowns all undertakings with success. OM obeisance to Chamunda who is the supreme goddess and whom illusion never touches and who grants all boon and crowns all undertakings with success. Om obeisance to the goddess Chamunda revealed in the shape of Koumari, obeisance to thee, O goddess, whose presence dispells the gloom of illusion and who grantest all boons and dost help all men to achieve success in their respective callings. Om obeisance to the goddess Gujhya (hidden) Kuvjika, destroy and destroy, O goddess, all the spells and incantations which my enemies have prepared or are preparing or will prepare in future against me. Trample down and reduce to ashes all banes which may befal me from the mystic diagrams which have been, or are being laid down by my enemies or will be ever laid down in future. Destroy and destroy them all, O thou goddess, looking doubly terrible with the rows of thy horrible teeth. Hrang, Hrung, Hung, obeisance to the goddess Gujhya Kuvjika. Hrung, Om, Khem, Vom, obeisance (Namas) to the goddess Gujhya, Kuvjika." Similarly should be recited the Mantras running as "Hreeng obeisance to the goddess, who afflicts all created beings. Hrung obeisance to the goddess who attracts the mind of all (Sarvajanakarshini)." Likewise, the Mantras running as "Am, Khem, obeisance to the goddess Sarvajanavashankari (the goddess who charms all beings) Om obeisance (Svaha) to the goddess Chamunda revealed as the wife of Vishnu (Vaishnavi), and whom illusion can never touch, and who grants all boon and success to her votaries. Om obeisance to the goddess Chamunda, who is the wife of the boar incarnation of Vishnu (Varaha) and who is omniscient and beyond all illusion and who grants all boon and success to her votaries. Om obeisance to the goddess Chamunda who is also revealed as the queen of the gods (Indrani) and whose very presence rends as under the veil of illusion and grants all boon and success to her worshippers. Om obeisance to the omniscient Chamunda who is the wife of the god Chanda (Chundi) and who is void of all illusion and grant all success to her suppliants, and Om obeisance to the goddess Chamunda who is the wife of the god Ishana (Ishani) and as such is omniscient, free from all illusion, and grants all boon and success to her votaries."

An equal number of terms appertain to the part of the present Mantra held sacred to the god Vishnu and which is as follows:—"Om obeisance to the goddess Chamunda on the burning crown of whose head the flaming hairs stand on their roots and from whose hung-down tongue drops the liquid lightning rendering the face look doubly angry with the starry eyes overhung with flame-coloured eyebrows and rows of horrible teeth exposed in ghastly laughter. Om laugh and laugh, O thou goddess, who art fond of wine and relishest human flesh and blood. Om, dance and dance, Om, yawn and yawn, Om, bind and bind down. Am, to the thousands of whose sorceresses who change the aspects of the three worlds through their fell spells and incantations. Om, thrash and thrash, Om, grind and cleanse, Om, O thou whose presence strikes terror into the breast of all created beings, Om, O thou who art terror of the three worlds (Trasini),

Om, O thou who dost move and give fresh impetus to the ever changing universe (Brahmini), Om, O thou who dost melt and melt (Dravini), agitate and agitate, destroy and destroy and revive and revive the universe. Heri, Heri, Geri, Geri, Gheri, Gheri, Om, Mari, Mari, Om obesiance to the Matris" (I-4).

The Trikhandi Mantra sacred to the god Shiva consists of the Beejas "Ha," "Ghou" preceded and followed by the five Pranava Mantras, which should be repeated and worshipped on the proper occasion. The Mantra known as the "Kuvjik Hridaya" and which consists of the Mantras "Ha," "Ghou" should be placed in the middle of the Mantra followed by the three "Akuladi" and the Madhyastha Mantras. The Akula Mantras as well as the different manifestations of the goddess of energy known as "Sashini" (the goddess or the energy revealed in the moon), Bhanuni (the divine energy manifest in the sun), Pavini (divine energy as revealed in the fire) together with the goddess Gandhari of whose essence the letter "Na" is the symbol and the goddesses known as Pindakshi, Chapala and Gajajihvika should be worshipped on the mystic diagram (Mandala). Similarly the goddess Mrisa, Bhayasara (whose divine attributes are represented by the Mantra "Ma," Madhyama (the emblem of whose divinity is the Mantra "Fa") Ajara, Kumari' Kalaratri (represented by the Mantra "Na"), Sankata (whose divine attributes are symbolised by the Mantra "Da"), Kalika represented by the letter "Dha," Shiva (represented by the letter "Fa.") Bhavaghora (the goddess who represents the necessary cycles of existence on this miserable terrestrial globe and accordingly strikes terror into the hearts of the inmates three worlds and whose divine attributes are symbolised in Murdhanya

"N" of the Sanskrit alphabet). Vibhatsa (the terrible goddess represented by the letter "Dha"), Viduta (the goddess or energy revealed in the flash of lightning and represented by the letter "Ta"), Vishambara (the goddess or the energy serving as the main stay of the universe and represented by the letter "Dha.") Shanshinis (the goddess who is revealed in the energy of doubt and represented by the letter "Edha'). Karali (the goddess of ugliness) Jvalamala (the goddess or the energy revealed in the conflagration which will burn the universe at the time of its dissolution), Durjaya (the invincible energy), Rangi (the aportive energy). Vama, Jestha (representing with the former goddess the two opposite polarities of the divine energy). Kali (the goddess of energy regulating the order of eternal time and represented by the letter "Kha"), Kulalamvi (the goddess or energy regulating the due succession of events and represented by the letter "Ka") Anuloma, Pindini (the goddess or the energy regulating the co-operation of the three primordial forces of Sattva, Rajas and Tamas and accordingly helping the conglomeration of the molecules of matter and represented by the letter "Da"), Vedini (the goddess or the energy revealed as pain and represented by the letter 'A'), Shantimurti (the imaged Peace, of which the letter 'E' is the symbol), Khadgini (the sword wielding goddess represented by the letter "Ri") and the goddesses Valita and Kula respectively represented by the letters "U" and "Lri," should be as well worshipped within the circumference of the diagram and in due succession with the goddesses Subhaga, Vedana, Karali, etc., who are known as the Madhyamas and the goddess Apetaraya respectively symbolised by the conjuncts Am and As" (5-11).

"Spham, Skheem, Skhoum, obeisance to the great Bhairava." The goddesses named as Akshodya (some editions read Akshobhyas), Rikshakarni, Rakshasi, Kshapanakshya, Akshaya, Kshema, Pingakshi and Brahmani, constitute the group of Brahmanies. The goddess Ila (goddess of fleeting fortune), Lilavati (the sportive goddesses), Neela, Lanka, Lankeshvari, Lalasa (desire), Vimala (purity), and Mala constitute what is known as the group of the Maheshvaris (the supreme goddess). The goddesses named as Hutashana (fire goddess), Vishalakshi (goddess with a pair of large and handsome eyes) Hrunkari, Vadavamukhi (the goddess from whose mouth volcanic flames are supposed to be emitted as found in ocean beds) Ha-Ha-rava (the goddess of wailing). Krura (the goddess of cruelty) Krodha (the goddess of warth). Vala, (the goddess of feminine grace), Kharamukha (the goddess with the face of an ass) are known to have emanated from the body of the goddess Koumari (the goddess of virginity) and who grant all boons to their votaries, if duly worshipped and propitiated. The goddess Sarvajna (the goddess of omniscience), Tarala (the goddess of lightning), Tara (the goddess of emancipation), Rig Veda, (the goddess of the Rig Veda), Hayanana (the goddess with a horse's head, Sara (the goddess of strength) Sara Sayangraha (the goddess who separates and picks up the merit or substance from the demerit, or the unsubstantial part), and Shashvati (the goddess of eternity) belong to the group of the Vaishnavis. The goddess such as Talajihva, Raktakshi, Vidyujjihva, Karankini, Meghananda, Prachandogra, Kalakarni, Kalipriya belong to the group of Varahi and should be worshipped by a votary with a view to achieve success in a military expedition. The goddesses named as Chanda Chandavati, Prachanda, Jvalitanana, Pichuvaktra and Lolupa have emanated from the body of the goddess Aindri. The goddesses such as Pavani, Jachani, Vamani, Damani, Vindunila, Vrihatkushi, Vidyuta and Vishvarupini belong to the class of Chamunda and should be worshipped inside the periphery of the mystic diagram with a view to win victories in war. The goddesses Jamajihya (the goddess on whose tongue sits the god of death), Jayanti (the goddess of victory), Durjava (the invincible goddess), and Jamantika, Vidali, Revati, Jaya, and Vijaya belong to the class of Mahalakhmis, in groups of eight (12-21).

"Obeisance to the goddess who subjugates the mind of all persons. Am Kshoum obeisance to the goddess who stupefies the faculties of all. Em, Khem, Khvam, obeisance to the goddess Kshovani." The nine Tvarita Mantras (Mantras sacred to the goddess Tvarita) run as "Fam, Shrung, Ksheeng, Shreem, Hreem, Khem, Vaccha, Ksha, Kshe, Hrun Fut, Hreen, obeisance, Om Hrun, Kshe, Vacche, Kshe, Kshee, Hreen, Fut." The seat should be spread out by repeating the Mantra which runs as "Hreem (obeisance) to the celestial lion" (the goddess rides upon). The Mantra Hreem Kshe should be located in the region of the heart, while the votary should locate in his head the Mantra running as "Obeisance (Svaha) Vaccha." The rite of Nyasa in connection with the worship of the goddess Tvarita should be performed as follows:—Kshem, Hreem, obeisance (Vashat), to the principles represented by the foregoing Veeja Mantras imagined as situated in my head. Obeisance to the principles represented by the Beeja Mantra Kshem, Houm which protects me as my armour. Obeisance (Voushat) to the principle of which the Mantra Hrum located in my three eyes, is the symbol, while the rite should be closed by repeating the Mantra Hreeng Fut. The nine Shaktis or the goddesses of energy whose divine virtues are represented by the Mantra Hum and whose respective essences serves to make it such a potent factor in the worship of the goddess are named as Hrinkari, Khechari, Chanda, Chedini, Kshovani, Kriya, Kshemakari, Hreenkari (sic) and Futkari (1-5).

Now I shall enumerate the names of the deities or the companions of the goddess Tvarita who are to be worshipped in the different angular points of the mystic diagram commencing with the one situate at the east as follow:—"Hreen obeisance to the goddess Nala possessed of extremely thick lips (Vahutunda) and high cheek bones and who travels through the skies. Hreen to the goddess whose thoroughfare is the infinite expanse of ether itself and who is manifest as an embodied conflagration. Burn and Burn, Oh, thou goddess Kha, Khe, Chachha, Oh thou, whose deathlike ghastly countenance does inspire terror into the hearts of men. Oh thou terrible looking wife of the god Chanda, who cuttest everything that comes in thy way. Kha, Khe, Chachhe, Shve, Oh thou goddess, whose embodiments are the principles represented by the Mantras Kha, Ra, Ha, Hring. Again I utter the Manta Kshe Oh thou goddess Kapila, Ha, Kshe, Hrung, Krang, Oh thou mother Roudri, who art resplendent with thy own celestial energy and splendour. Hreen, Fe, Va, Fa, Fa, Vakra, Vari Fe, Puti Puti, to thee Oh goddess, who art the personified gloom that would prevail at the time of universal dissolution. Hrung Fut to thee Oh goddess, who art encircled by the Brahmavetalas (a class of goblins.)"

Now I shall again enumerate the secret Mantras held sacred to the goddess Tvarita. The rite of secret Nyasa should by performed as follows:- "Obeisance to the principles represented by the Mantras Hroun, Houn and Has which are located in the region of my heart. Obeisance to the principles symbolised by the Mantras Houn and Has and which are situated in the substance of my brain. May the Mantra running as Fe Jvala illuminate the part of my body occupied by the tuft of hair on my crown, and may the Mantras Hran, Hun, Han Ila, protect me as my armour with the virtue of the principle they stand for. May the Mantras Kroun, Kshoum, Shreen together with the principles they are emblematic of, be located in my eyes, and may the Mantras running as Kshoun, Houn, Fut serve me as a weapon. In the alternative, the Mantra would run as Hnu, Kshe, Va, Cha, Kshes, Hrun, Kshen, Hnu, Fut, Oh thou wife of the ever-blissful deity (Sadashiva). The Mantra Kshe should be uttered in the beginning and Hrun in the middle. The letter Va stands for the god Isha, the Mantra Chache is emblematic of the divinity of the deity known as Manonmani, Ma and Kshe are the symbols of the celestial Garuda, while the Mantra Hrun represents the divine attributes of the god Madhava. The Mantra Kshem stands for the god Brahma, Hnu represents the sun-god while the Fut should be known as the weapon Mantra (6-9).

VI

THE MOST MYSTERIOUS OF THE SIN EXPIATING RITES

Pushkara said:—

Now I shall describe the most mysterious of the sin-expiating rites, whereby a man would attain purity. A Mahapataki would be absolved of his sin by reciting the Pourusha Shukta for a month; while by thrice repeating the Aghamarshana Mantra, a sinner becomes free of all demerits. By repeating the Veda Mantras or the Mantras respectively sacred to the gods of wind and death, as well as by means of a Gayatri Vrata, a similar result is obtained (1-2).

In all forms of the penance known as the Krichchha Vrata, a penitent should shave his head, bathe, perform a Homa ceremony, and worship the God Hari. He should pass the day in a standing posture, and the night, seated. This is what is technically known as the Virasana. The practiser of a Krichchha Vrata, should adopt the Virasana posture during the continuance of his penance, whereby he would be absolved of his sin. A Yoti should practise a Chandrayana Vrata by taking eight morsels of food each day, while in the Vrata known as the "Shishu Chandrayana," he should take four moresels of food in the morning and evening. In the Vrata known as the Sura-Chandrayana, an anchorite will not be allowed to take more than two hundred and thirty four morsels of food during a period of two months. In a Tapta krichchha penance, the penitent shall live on three handsful of warm water for the first three days, on three handsful of warm milk for the second three days, on three handsful of warm clarified butter for the third three days, and on air for the last three days, water, milk, clarified butter being taken cold, even when the penance would be practised in a cold season. In the penance known as the Krichchhati-krichchha, the diet should be composed of milk, cowdung, urine of a cow, thickened milk, clarified butter, curd and washings of the blades of holy kusha grass for a period of twenty-one days. The Krichchha Santapana Vrata enjoins a fast for a whole day and night, while that having become through practice a matter of daily habit, constitutes what is known as the Maha Santapana Vrata, and such a fast being observed for three consecutive days constitute what is known as the Ati Santapana Vrata. In a Paraka Yajna, the period of fasting is extended to twelve days. In the Prajapatya form of the penance, the penitent should eat once a day for three consecutive days, and in the night, too, if any thing is obtained without asking for it. A Pada krichcha is the same as a Krichchha Vrata, save that its duration is less than that of the latter by a quarter (3-11).

In the penance known as the Phala Krichccha, a penitent should live on fruits for a month; while in the Shri Krichchha form, he should eat Bael fruits only during that period. In the Padmaksha form of penance, the diet should be composed of Amalakams only for a month, while in the Pushpa Krichccha form, the penitent should live on flowers only, during its continuance. In the penances known as the Patra Krichchha Toyas Krichchha, and Mula Krichchha, the diet should consist of leaves of trees, water, edible roots mixed with curd, thickened milk, or whey respectively. The penance known as the Vayavya which destroys all sin, should be practised by eating a handful of boiled rice each day for a month. The rite of expiation of sin known as the Krichchham-Agneyam should be practised by eating a handful of sessamum orientale each day, during a period of twelve days. In the penance known as the Brahma Kurcha, the diet should consist of fried paddy for a fortnight. A man having fasted on the fourteenth day of a fortnight, should eat the composition known as the Panchagavya, on the day following, and take no animal diet subsequent thereto. By doing the above-said penance twice a month, a man is absolved of all sins. A man with a view to acquire wealth and prosperity to purse off all sins, or to secure a passport to heaven after death, should practise the penance known as the Krichchha Vrata, whereby all his objects would be realised (12-17).

PUSHKARA SAID:—A man is naturally inclined to covet the wives and goods of his neighbours, or to kill animals in wanton cruelty, atonement for which should be made by constantly hymnising the Supreme Vishnu as follows:—"Obeisance to Vishnu and Vishnu, and to none but Vishnu. I make obeisance to Vishnu, who abiding in my heart, forms the sense of my egoism, and who is the lord of the universe, though himself invisible and lying latent behind this phenomenal world. Salutation unto Vishnu who is eternal, and uncontrolled by any incident or being,- the originless, deathless lord of all. Since Vishnu resides in my heart, since my intellection is carried on through the medium of his infinite intelligence, since Vishnu makes up the sum-total of differentiated egoistic existences, and since I dwell in him as a part and parcel of the universe, and since he is formed of the acts of beings, may my sins be absolved by my meditating upon his infinite purity. I stand a suppliant at the feet of that Hari, by contemplating whose divine self, a man is purged of all sin, whether due to wicked dreams or thought, and who wipes away all misery and affliction from the face of the Universal Nature. I make obeisance to Vishnu, who stoops down to the miserable sinners, ever falling down and down in the bottomless abyss of darkness, and lends a helping hand to lift them from irretrievable ruin. I make obeisance to thee, O Hrishikesha, O Hrishikesha, O Hrishikesha, who art the lord of the universe and (dost reign as) the Supreme Soul, though unperceived by the senses. Obeisance to thee, O thou Infinite Spirit (Ananta), O thou Govinda, (protector of the universe), O thou Nrisinha, O thou, who formest the subject of thought of the created beings. O thou Keshava, subdue and subdue my wicked thoughts and put an end to my misdeeds. O Keshava, set at naught whatever evil I have cherished in my mind at the dictates of my wicked heart, whatever fierce and diabolical acts I have planned in my mind, and pardon me for indulging therein. O thou Universal God, O thou Govinda, O thou Lord of the Universe (Jagannatha), O thou contemplated by the Universal Nature, O thou who formest the supreme end in life, destroy my sin. O thou Madhava, O thou Hrishikesha, O thou lotus-eyed god (Pundarikaksha), may my sins, whether committed in the morning, evening, noon, or in any other part of day, whether committed in sleep, dream or waking, whether committed by mind, body, or speech, be pardoned through the merit of repeating the three holy names of yours, stated above.

May the sins which have been committed through my body, mind or speech together with those committed in sleep, dream, or in the state of waking, whether at the time of sitting, resting, eating, or walking be all pardoned (1-15).

Oh thou Hrishikesha, Oh thou Madhava, possessed of the lotus like eyes, destroy all my sins whether committed by my limbs or by my speech. Destroy all my sins, whether committed by my body, mind or speech, whether incidental to my eating animal or unclean food, whether due to evil thoughts indulged in by me, while awake, or to lascivious dreams dreamt by me in sleep. Pardon, Oh God, all the delinquincies I am guilty of, either while going or at rest. May all those sins, whether due to my physical or intellectual existence, and by which I am sure to be doomed to the eternal torments of hell or to a low birth in my next existence be atoned for and pardoned by my constantly repeating the name of the god Vasudeva, in one continuous song of full-throated ease. I singingly repeat the name of Vishnu, who is the Supreme Brahma, the abode of the highest, holiest bliss. May all my sins be pardoned. The feet (god-head) of Vishnu, which are beyond all material principles such as those of sound, smell, touch, etc., and even beyond the comprehension of the gods, destroy al sin. The man who recites the sin-destroying hymn stated above, becomes absolved of all sin, whether oral, mental or physical, gets rid of the evil influences cast by the malignant planets, and becomes merged in the divine essence of Vishnu, to the close of this life. Hence this sin-destroying Psalm (Aghamarshana) should be sung and repeated by a man who has committed any sin. Better it is, that atonements should be made and penances should be performed simultaneously with a repetition of this Aghamarshana prayer, whereby the reciter is sure to be absolved of all sin. Hence they should be performed and repeated with a view to attain enjoyment in this life and salvation in the next (16-21).

VII

THE OMKAR MANTRA

SAID THE GOD OF FIRE:—

That man is no other than the god Hari incarnate on earth, who fully understands the mystery of the Omkar Mantra. Therefore it is incumbent on a man to constantly recite the Pranava Mantra which heads the list of all its compeers in respect of merit and sanctity. All the other Mantas should be used preceded by the Pranava Mantra. That rite or ceremony only should be deemed as complete and properly done which has been closed by repeating the Pranava Mantra. The three Vyahriti Mantras of infinite virtues are preceded by the holy "Omkār" as well as the Tripadā and the Sāvitri Mantra which has emanated from the mouths of the four faced deity.

The man who having subjugated his senses, repeats every day for a year the Pranava Mantra, shakes off his mortal coil and is converted into the universal expanse of ether which is but another manifestation of Para Brahma. The Ekakshara (Om) is the Para Brahma himself and Prānyama is the best of austerities. There is no better Mantra than the Gāyatri, and truthfulness is better than a vow of silence. By seven times repeating the Gāyatri Mantra, a man becomes absolved of all sins, while a ten times repetition of the same mantra leads a man to heaven. The Mantra twenty times repeated leads a man to the region of Isha, while through the merit of repeating hundred and eight times the same Mantra, the soul of a man is safely borne across this ocean of life. The Gāyatri Mantra excels the Rudra and Kushmanda Mantras in merit and sanctity. No other Mantra is better than the Gayatri as far as the merit of repetition is concerned, and there is no better Mantra to offer libations with than the Vyahritis. Even a single foot or a single Rich of the Gāyatri carries enough sanctity to purge a man of impieties incidental to the commission of such heinous crimes as the murder of a Brahmana, drinking of intoxicating liquors, theft of gold weighing more than eighty Ratis or going unto the wives of his elders or preceptors, or unto women who are in his forbidden degree of consanguinity (1-9).

On having unwittingly or unwillingly committed any sinful act, a man should repeat the Gāyatri Mantra and perform the Homa ceremony with the seeds of sessamum orientale. In the alternative he should mentally recite the Gāyatri Mantra and observe a fast for a whole day and night. Even the killer of a cow or of a Brahmana, a patricide, a matricide, defiler of the beds of superior persons, a drunkard or a gold stealer, may purge off their sins by repeating a hundred thousand times the holy Gāyatri Mantra. In the alternative the committer of any of the above-said sins, may regain his original purity by bathing in water and by repeating a hundred times the Gāyatri Mantra under its surface. Similarly by drinking a cup of water consecrated hundred times with the Gāyatri Mantra, a man becomes absolved of all impieties. The Gāyatri Mantra hundred times repeated procures pardon for all light delinquincies, a thousand repetition of the same Mantra destroys sins incidental to the commission of offences known as the Upapātakas—1 (sins of the second degree), while a ten million repetition grants all boons to the repeater and confers on him sovereignty in this world and godhead in the next. A similar result may be also obtained by repeating the Gāyatri preceded and followed by the Omkar and running as "Om Bhurbhuva, etc., Om" (10-15).

The Rishi who composed the Gayatri or the rhapsodist who first sang its verse was Vishvāmitra. The metre of distich is Gāyatri. The presiding deity of the Mantra is the Sun-god, while it should be mentally repeated (Japa) or used (Viniyoga) in connection with casting libations of clarified butter into the sacrificial fire or on the occasion of appeasing the wraths of gods. The gods which preside over the different letters composing the distich, are the Fire-god, the god of wind, the Sun-god, the Lightning, the god of death, the god of the oceans, the Jupiter, the god of rain (Parjanaya), the king of the celestials (Indra), Gandharva, Pushā, Mitra, Varuna, Tvasta, the Vasus, the Marut, the Moon, the immortal sage Angira, Vasava, Nasati, Ka, Rudra, Brahma, Vishnu and the rest of the gods successively, who at the time of reciting the Mantra, jointly wipe away the sable sin from the soul of the repeater, engendered either through the instrumentality of toes, calves, legs, knee-joints, groins, genitals, scrotum, waist, belly, breasts, heart, neck, face, palate, nose, eyes, eye-brows, forehead, lips, the sides, the head, or the mouth. The colours which mark the body of the goddess Gāyatri, are yellow, blue, brown, emerald, flame-colour, golden, lightning colour, yellowish black, Black, blood-red, sapphire like, crystal, palegold, ruby, golden, brown, reddish blue, blackish-red, gold-shade, white, and blackish scarlet. The goddess should be contemplated as having a complexion variagated by the above-said colours. By meditating on the divine nature of the goddess and by casting libations of clarified butter into the fire in her honour, a man becomes purged of all sins (16-24).

A Homa ceremony performed with libations of clarified butter containing the seeds of seassamum orientale, and a repetition the Gāyatri Mantra, tends to absolve a man of all sins, while the Gāyatri Homas undertaken for the purposes of peace-making or for the prolongation of one's life, shall respectively consist of libations containing barley or clarified butter simply. For the realisation of one's own ends, the Gāyatri Homa should be performed with sundried rice, while the one undertaken with a view to become merged in the essence of Brahman, should consist of libations of sweetened porridge. A man inorder to have male issues should perform the Gāyatri Homa with libations of curd, while in the one performed for the increase of one's wealth, oblations of Shali-Rice should be cast into the sacrificial fire: Stems of Bilva trees should be offered as oblations in the one performed for the increase of one's wealth, while lotuses should be cast into the fire in the one performed for the purposes of increasing one's personal beauty. A man desirous of getting rid of a disease should perform a Gāyatri Homa with bunches of green grass, and similar oblations should be offered in the one undertaken with a view to quell all physical or social disturbances. The oblations should consist of scented gum resin in the one performed with a view to bring good luck, while the man who wishes to obtain a proficiency in learning, should perform a Gāyatri Homa by offering libations of sweetened porridge. By casting ten thousand libatons into the sacrificial fire, a man becomes possessed of the above- said superhuman powers (Siddhis), while by offering such hundred thousand, he will be able to realise all his heartfelt objects. By offering a million libations a man is absolved of the sin incidental to the murder of a Brahmana, becomes able to redeem the souls of all his relations and finally becomes one with the god Hari. The goddess Gāyatri should be invoked at the commencement of all sacrifices, performed for the propitiation of hostile planets or for any other purposes (25-30).

After that the performer of the Homa, should meditate upon the mystic significance of the Omkar, and tie up into a knot the tuft of hair on the crown of his head by once reciting the Gāyatri Mantra. Then he should again rinse his mouth with water and touch the regions of his shoulders heart and the umbilicus. The guardian saint (Rishi) of the Omkar is Brahmā, the metre of the verse is Gāyatri and its presiding deity is Agni. The Omkar is Paramātmā (the Supreme Soul) himself and should be used in all sorts of religious rites. The goddess adored in the three worlds, should be contemplated as possessed of a white complexion and seated on a full blown lotus flower and carrying a rosary. The goddess should be invoked as follows:- "Om thou art the light, the sacrifice, the strength, the seventh sun, the abode of the gods. The universe is thy self and thou fillest it with life and motion. Thou art the life of all and the duration—of all lives. Om to the Earth. Come, oh thou goddess, who grantest boon to thy votaries, and stay as long as I repeat thy holy name" (31-34).

Prajāpati is the composer or the first singer of the seven Vyahriti Mantras. The Omkar Mantra which respresents the essence of Para Brahma, occurs at the commencement of each of the several Vyahritis, as well as before the collected Vyahritis running as a single Mantra. The presiding gods or patron saints of the successive Vyahritis, are Vishvāmitra, Jamadagni, Bharadvāja, Gotama, Atri, Vashishtha, Kāshyapa, the god of fire, the Wind-god, the Sun-god, the Jupiter, Varuna, Indra and Vishnu. The metres of the Vyahritis are the Gāyatri, Ushnik, Anusthupa, Vrihati, Pankti, Tristupa, and the Jagati. The Vyahritis should be made use of in practising a Pranyama or in casting libations of clarified butter into the fire in connection with a Homa ceremony (35-39).

The man who sprinkles upward eight drops of water, by reciting the Mantras respectively running as "Apohistha" "Apām," "Drupadā," "Hirna Varna" and Pāvamāni, is sure to purge off all sins committed by him from the very moment of his birth. A Brahmana should repeat thrice under water, the Aghamarshana Mantra and the Mantra running as "Ritancha" etc. The Rishi who composed or first sang the Rich running as "Apohistā" etc., was Sindhudvipa. The metre of the Mantra is Gāyatri and the water is its presiding deity. The Mantra should be used at the time of ablution known as the Brahmasnānam and in dashing water over the body in a sacrificial bathing or at the time of bathing a horse in connection with a horse-sacrifice. The Rishi who composed or first sang this Aghamarshana Sukta (sin destroying verse) was Aghamarshana, the metre of the verse is Anustap and its presiding deity is Bhāvavritta. The Mantra running as "Apo Jyoti Rasa" etc., forms the head of the Gāyatri. The name of its Rishi is Prajāpati, no metre being used in its composition, as Yajus is not metrical. The presiding deities of the verses are Brahma, Agni, Vayu, and the Sun. The wind is generated within the body of the reciter by the suppression of the breath, which in its turn produces fire and out of fire water is produced, wherewith the reader of the verse should rinse his mouth. The Rishi who composed or first sang the Mantra running as "Udityam Jāta Vedasam" was Praskanna. The metre of the verse is Gāyatri, while its presiding deity is the sun-god. The Mantra should be used on the occasion of an Atirātra sacrifice. Koutsa is the composer of or the first Rhapsodist who sang the Rich running as Chitram Devati. The metre of the verse is Tristup and the sun is its presiding god (40-49).

VIII

THE GAYATRI MANTRA

SAID THE GOD OF FIRE:—

Thus having performed the rite of his daily Sandhya, a Brahmana should recite the Gāyatri Mantra running as "Om Bhurbhuva Sva, Tat Saviturvarenyam Bhargo Devasya Dhemahi, Dheo No Prachodāyāt Om." The Mantra is called the Gāyatri (lit, an emancipating song) from the fact of its delivering the singers and their wives from the cycle of re-births. Since its essence serves to illumine the sun (Savita) and forms the fountain source of all light in the universe, it is also known as the Sāvitri Mantra. Since it first came as a word out of the mouth of the four-faced deity it is also called the Sarasvati. The word "Bharga" occurring in the middle of the Mantra represents the supreme light, the essence of the Para Brahma, from the root Bha to shine and Bhrasja to cook or ripen, in which sense it has been used many times in the Chandas (Vedas). The word refers to that essence of the god which causes the cereals to ripen in the harvest time and dispels the gloom of night which enveloped the universe before the dawn of creation. The light-essence of the Supreme Being is the mightiest of all lights, and this self of the universal Spirits is the most adored (Varenyam) of all existences. In the alternative it may mean that the divine self of the Absolute should be worshipped with a view to ensure a heavenly existence. And since the root Vri of the term Varenyam may also mean "to cover," it necessarily signifies, as used in the text, an existence which envelopes or lies beyond the states of waking, sleeping, and dreaming and hence a Being who is changeless, eternal and absolutely pure—the Universal God, the Absolute Purity, the Perfect Knowledge, the Infinite Reality. For the emancipation of my soul, I meditate upon the divine self of that light which is the god Vishnu, the origin of the universe. Some there are who read "Shiva," "Shakti," "Agni" (such as the Agni Hotris) in the place of "light" in the text of the Mantras. And since the term Vishnu has been described in the Vedas and the other holy scriptures as synonymous with the sun the fire, and the Rudra, it makes no essential difference, which ever of these epithets has been used. The divine-self of that god, manifest as the sun or Vishnu, produces the libations of clarified butter, and it is the self same god manifests as the light, Prajanya (the god of rain), Vayu (the wind), Aditya (the sun) grows and nourishes the cereals and vegetables by giving rise to heat and moisture. Libations of clarified butter cast into the fire are carried to the sun who creates the rain-clouds. Rain causes the stalks of food grains (Annam) to shoot out and man is the offspring of food (Annam) (1-11).

The word "Dhimahi," in the text may be also derived from the root "Dha" to hold; and accordingly the Mantra may be interpreted to mean "may we make a full comprehension of the god who is the creator of the seven regions known as the Bhuh, Bhubas, etc. The word Nas is the possessive plural form of the personal pronoun "I," and the word "Bharga" means divinity or divine essence; and hence the latter part of the Mantra (Bhago Devasya Prachodyat means:— "May that essence of the god Vishnu manifest as the sun or the fire-god, lead the minds of us (all created beings) to dwell on his divine self in all acts and undertakings and at all times. Led by the god, the soul of a man goes to heaven or falls into the pit of this material universe which is nothing but the cavity of the mouth of Hari. A Brahmana should hold himself identical with the god who sports on the fields of paradise. A Yogi bent on working out the salvation of his soul, shall behold the essence of the universal spirit reflected in the disc of the sun, at the sight of which he would break the chain of births and deaths, and get rid of the three sorts of pain a man is usually heir to and recite the following Mantras:-

"You are that eternal Brahma, the infinite spiritual light, O thou who shinest in the disc of the sun. I am identical with thee, O thou the divinity of Vishnu! The states of waking, sleep, or dreaming do not constitute my self. I am beyond these. I am a dis-embodied spirit filling the universal space and running through all sorts of life up to the Supreme Brahma. I deem myself on with the absolute spirit, the Aditya Purusha. I am the infinite and eternal "Om," whence flows out all knowledge and good deeds" (12-18).

IX

THE USE OF THE GAYATRI MANTRA FOR WORSHIPPING THE PHALIC EMBLEM

SAID THE GOD OF FIRE:—

The holy sage Vashishtha became an adept in Yoga by worshipping the phalic emblem of Shiva by reciting the Gāyatri Mantra, while the latter and other sages attained salvation and became merged in the Supreme Brahma by worshipping the same divine emblem. Vashishtha propitiated the god with the following prayer. "I make obeisance to thy emblem of creation, O lord, as manifest in gold (Kanakalinga, lit:—a golden phalic emblem), obeisance to thy emblem of creative energy as unfolded in the holy Vedas, obeisance to thy supreme emblem, obeisance to thy image as manifest in the universal expanse of ether. Obeisance to thy divine essence emblematized by thousands and thousands of symbols. Obeisance to thy creative energy as manifest in the fire, obeisance to thy creative energy which manifests itself in the composition of the Puranams. Obeisance to thy creative essence which has embodied itself in the truths of the Shrutis. Obeisance to thy creative potency as manifest in the nether regions (Pātālas). Obeisance to thy creative emblem which is known as the Supreme Brahma. Obeisance to thy mysterious emblem of creation which lies beyond the ken of human beings. Obeisance to thy creative essence which is spread all over the seven continents of the world. Obeisance to thy creative essence symbolised by the collective souls of the universe. Obeisance to thy creative energy which is emblematised by the limbs and organs of animals. Obeisance to thy emblem of creative energy which lies latent in Nature. Obeisance to thy creative essence symbolised by the process of intellection. Obeisance to thy creative potency represented by the egoistic senses of sentient creatures. Obeisance to thy creative essences symbolised by the material principles. Obeisance to thy creative energy of which the proper sensible are the symbols. Obeisance to the creative energy which determines the subjective principles in individuals. Obeisance to thy creative potency manifest in the dynamical forces of sentiments. Obeisance to thy creative potency which is above the virtue of Rajas (universal cohesion) and is known as the Satva Guna. Obeisance to thy creative agency manifest in acts of becoming. Obeisance to thy creative energy manifest in the combined action of the three universal forces of Satva, Raja and Tamas (Adhesion, cohesion, and disintegration). Obeisance to thy creative energy represented by futarity (Probability). Obeisance to thy creative energy manifest in the shape of heat and light. Obeisance to thy creative energy which works in regions beyond the zone of atmosphere. Obeisance to thy creative energy which has embodied itself in the mighty truths of the Shrutis. Obeisance to thy creative energy represented by truths inculcated in the Atharva Mantras and the psalms of the holy Sama Veda. Obeisance to thy creative essence which manifests itself in the shape of a religious sacrifice, and the different rites (Yajnanga) constituting the same. Obeisance to thy creative essence which forms the fundamental principles and the immutable truths of the universe. Help us, O God, in reaching the extreme goal of the Yoga. Bless me with the birth of son equal to me in every respect. May we attain the Supreme Brahma. May the virtue of self-control never leave us. May there be not a gap in the line of our descendants, and may our faith in religion and in thy absolute goodness never be weakened" (1-11).

SAID THE GOD OF FIRE:- The holy sage Vashishtha thus propitiated of yore the self-origined deity on the summit of the mountain Shriparvata, and the god gave him a boon and went away pleased with his devotion (12).

X

THE MANTRAS TO BE USED ON THE OCCASION OF THE INSTALLATION OF A KING

PUSHKARA SAID:-

Now I shall narrate the Mantras which are to be used on the occasion of the installation of a king or an idol, and which are potent enough to destroy al sorts of sin. The water on the occasion should be kept in pitchers and sprinkled over with the blades of Kusha grass, whereby all the purposes of ablution or washing would be served. The Mantra runs as follows:—"May the gods such as Brahma, Vishnu, Maheshvara, Vāsudeva, Sankarshana. Pradumnya and Aniruddha, install you in full glory by pouring water on your head. May the gods and celestial beings such as the Manus, the Dikpālas, Rudra, Dharma, Ruchi, Shraddhā lead you to victory. May the holy saints Bhrigu, Atri, Vashishtha, Sanaka, Sanandana, Sanat Kumara, Angira, Pulasta, Pulaha, Kratu, Marichi, Kashyapa, the Prajapatis, the god Kārtickeya and the Pitris known as the Agnishvattas preserve you. May the demons (Kravyadas), Ajyapas, and Sukālis preserve you. May the goddesses such as Lakshmi and the wives of the god of virtue, as well as the consorts of Kushyapa, the father of many sons, of Krishāshva, of Aristanemi, of Agniputra Ashvini and the other wives of the moon god and the beloved wives of Pulaha preserved you. May Aruna, the charioter of the sun and the celestial matrons known as Bhutā, Kapishā Danstri, Surasā Saramā, Danu, Shyani, Bhāsi, Krounchi, Dhritarastri and Shuki install you in full glory by pouring down water on your head. May the goddess Ayati (goddess of futarity), Niyati (fate), Rātri (night) and Nidrā (sleep) who exist for the advancement of the human race, as well as the goddess Umā, Menā, Shachi, Dhumornā, Niriti, Jayā, Gouri, Shivā, Riddhi, Velā, Avā, Asikni and Jyotsna, and the Kalpas, Mahakalpas (cycles of time), the Manvantaras, the years, the Samvatsaras, the Yugas, the movements of the sun, the divisions of the year such as the seasons, the months, the fortnights, the weeks, the day, the evening, the days of the lunar months,

Sacred words of Power

the Muhurtās (a period of 48 minutes), the sun with his planets and satellites, preserve you. May the fourteen Manus such as Sāyambhuba, Svārochisha, Outtama, Tāmasa, Revata. Chakshusha, Vaivasvata, Sāvarna, Brahm-putra, Dharmaputra, Rudraja, Dakshaa, Rouchya and Bhoutya, and the principal gods, such as Vishvabhuk, Vipatti, Shuchiti, Shikhi, Vibhu, Manojava, Ojashvi, Vali, Adbhuta, Shānti, Vrisha, Rita-dharmā, Divasprik, Kāma, Indraka, Ravanta, Kumara, Vatsa, Vināyaka, Vira, Chandra, Nandi, Vishvakarmā, Purorava, come and take part in this thy coronation ceremony. May the twin Ashvini Kumāras- the physicians of heaven, the eight Vasus (demi-gods) such as Dhruva, etc., the ten Angirasas and the Vedas put the crown on thy head and lead thee to victory. May the soul, duration of life, mind, vitality, egoism, Rita and truth preserve thee. May Kratu, Daksha, Vasu, Satya, Kālakāma and Dhuri lead thee to victory. May the gods, Pururava, Mādrava, Vishedevas, Rochana, Angarakas, the Sun-god, Nirita, Yama, Ajaikapada, Ahirvradhna, the comets, the Rudrajas, Bharata, the death, Kapāli, Kinkini, Bhavana, Bhāvana, Svajanas and their wives, Kratushravā, Murdha, Yājnatishana, Prasava, Abhaya Daksha, the Bhrigus, the Prānas, the nine Apanās, Vitihotra, Naya, Sādhya, Hansa and Nārāyana preserve thee. May the superior members of the celestial hierarchy who are devoted to the good of the universe, such as Vibhu, Prabhu, and the twelve Bhaskaras such as Dhātā, Mitra, Aryamā, Pusha, Shakra, Varuna, Bhaga, Tasta, Vivasvāna, Savitā and Vishnu, as well as Ekajyotis, Dvijyotis, Trijyotis, Chaturjyotis, Ekashakra, Dvishakra, Trishakra, Mitra, Sanmita, Amita, Ritajit, Satyajit, Sushena, Senajit, Atimitra, Anumitra, Purumitra, Aparājita, Ritā. Ritavak, Dhāta, Vidhāta, Dhārana, Dhruva and Vidharama, the mighty colleagues of the king of the gods, preserve thee (1-31).

May the holy Rishis who are the practisers of the most austere penances, such as Idriksha, Adriksha, Etadriksha, Amitāshana, Kridita, Sadriksha, Sharabha, Dharta, Dhurya, Dhuri, Bhima, Abhibhukta, Kshapasaha, Dhriti, Vasu, Anādhrishya, Rama, Kama, Jaya, Virata, as well as the forty-nine wind-gods preserve thee (32-34).

May the Gandharvas such as Chitrangada, Chitraratha, Chitrasena, Kali, Unāyu, Ugrasena, Dhritarāshatra, Nandaka, Hāhā, Huhu, Nārāda, Vishāvasu and Tumvaru, install thee in full glory and lead thee to victory. May the celestial beauties such as Anavadyā, Sukeshi, Menakā, Sahajanyā, Kratusthali, Gritāchi, Vishvāchi, Punjakasthali, Pramlochā, Urvashi, Ramābhā, Panchachudā, Tilottamā, Chitralekhā, Lakshmanā, Pundarikā, and Vāruni, as well as the demons Pralhada, Virochana, Vali, Vana and his sons and the Rakshases come and install thee in full glory. May the Siddhas, Yakshas, and the celestial gems, accompanied by Nandana, Manibhadra, Schandana, Pingāksha, Dyutimāna, Puspavāna, Jayavaha, lead thee to victory. May the Pishachas led by their chiefs such as Urdhakesha, and the ghosts who dwell in earth, come and take part in this inauguration ceremony, following in the train of the Matris, Narasinha, Mahākala, Guha and Skandha. May the celestial Garuda, with other principal celestial birds such as Aruna and Sampāti, as well as the primordial Hydra (Vāsuki) and the serpents Takshaka, and the celestial elephants Airavata, Mahapadma, Shankha, Puspadanta, Vāmana, etc., always protect thee from (35-49).

Sacred words of Power

May the celestial swan the god Brahma rides upon and the bull of the god Shankara, the lion of the goddess Durga, the buffalo of the god of death, the horse Ucchaishrava belonging to Indra, the celestial Kousthuva, the lord of the conch shells, the thunder-bolt, the celestial mace, the discus, and other weapons preserve thee. May the gods Chitragupta, Danda, Pingala, Mrityu and Kāla preserve thee. May the souls of Munis such as Vyasa, Vālmiki and the Valakhilyas preserve thee. May the souls of departed kings such as Prithu, Dilipa, Bharata, Dushmanta, Shakrajit, Vali, Malla. Kukutstha, Anena, Juvānāshva, Jayadhratha, Māndhāta, Muchukunda and Pururavā preserve thee. May the gods of the homestead and the twenty-five fundamental principles of the universe lead thee to victory. May the regions of golden soil, sandy soil, yellow soil, white soil, and of yellowish red soil, the Pātala, the Rasātala, the regions known as the Bhu, Bhuva, lead the to victory. May the continents of Jamvudvipa, the Northern Kuru Hiranyaka Bhadrāshva, Ketumāla, Valāhaka, Haivarsha, Kimpurusha, Indradvipa, Kasherumāna, Tamraparna, Gabhastimana, Nāgadvipa, Soumyaka, Gandharbha and Varuna preserve thee. May the mountains known as the Himavana, the Hemakuta, the Nishadha, the Nila, the Shāveta, the Shringavana, the Meru, the Mālyavana, the Gandhamādana, the Mahendra, the Malaya, the Sajhya, the Shaktimāna, the Rikshavāna, the Vindhya and the Paripātra grant thee peace (50-57).

May the holy Vedas such as the Rik etc., with their six branches of kindred sciences, the books of history, the Puranas, the Medical sciences, the sciences of music and war, the sciences of proper pronunciation, ritual, grammar, lexicon, astronomy and prosody, the six schools of philosophy such as the Sankhya, the Yoga, the Mimansa, the Naya, etc., the schools of philosophy known as the Pāshupatam and the Pancharātrum, the Gāyatri Mantras respectively sacred to the god Shiva and the goddesses Durga, Vidya and Gandhari grant thee peace. (58-62).

May the four oceans of sugarcane juice, clarified butter, curd and milk, as well as the holy places and pools such as the cities of Pushkara, Prayāga, Prabhāsa, the forest of Naimisha, the shrines of Gayashirsha, Brahmashirsha, the Northern Mānasa, the Kālodaka, the Nandikunda, the land of the five rivers, the Bhrigu Tirtha, the Amarakantakam, Jambu Marga, the hermitage of Kapila, the source of the Ganges, Kushavarta, the Vindhyaka, the Nila Parvata, the Varaha Parvata, Kankhalam, Kālanjar, Kedar, Rudrakoti, Benares, the hermitage of Vayasa (Vadarjyashrama), Dwarka, the Shri mountain, Purushottama, the village of Shālagrama, Karavirāshrama, the junctions of rivers with the seas, the river Phalgu, the Vindusara, the Ganges, the Sarasvati, the Shatadru, the Gandaki, the Achchohda, the Vipāshā, the Nischirā, the Gomati, the Parā, the Charmanvati, the Rupā, the Mandākini, the Mahānadi, the Tāpi, the Payoshni, the Venā, the Gouri, the Vaitarani, the Godāvari, the Bhimarathi the Tungabhadrā, the Prāni, and the Chandrabhāgā, preserve and install thee in full glory. (63-72).

XI

THE RITES MANTRAS OF THE SAMA VEDA

PUSHKARA SAID:—

I have done with the rites and Mantas which appertain to the Yajur-veda, now I shall describe those which belong to the Saman. A man, by repeating the Sanhita known as the Vaishnabi, is sure to witness the realisation of all his wished—for objects. O thou of exemplary conduct, a man by repeating the Chhandasi Sanhita, is sure to win the good graces of the god Shankara, while by repeating those respectively known as the Paitri and the Skandi, a man is sure to enjoy the greatest self-complacence. A repetition of the Mantras running as Indram Bhajamahe (we worship the god Indra), destroys the evil effects of dreadful incantations practised against a man. A man in prison, would be liberated by repeating the Mantra running as Agni Stigma, etc. A man having committed the sin of selling improper articles, should repeat the Mantra running as Ghritavati etc. A repetition of the Mantra running as Ayāno Deva Savitri, etc., tends to neutralise the effects of a bad dream (1-5).

O thou best of the sons of Bhrigu, a woman suffering from repeated miscarriages, should use clarified butter consecrated with the Mantras running as Avodya Agni, etc., and by tieing a girdle of threat round her waist with the Mantras running as Abhukshya, etc. The tuft of hair on the crown of a new-born babe, should be tied up with the Mantra running as Somam Rajanam, whereby he would be free of all diseases. A man, by constantly reciting the Sarpa Saman, becomes safe from snake-bites. A Brahmana, by casting a thousand libations of clarified butter with the Mantra of Medhya, etc., and by tieing up the tuft of hair on his crown with it, is sure to enjoy an immunity from swordcuts, or from blows of weapons in general. Similarly, by performing a Homa ceremony with the Mantra known as the Dirgha Tamasorka, a man is sure to have plenty of boiled rice every day. A man, by repeating the Mantra running as Svamadhyanti etc., never dies of thirst. Similarly, by repeating the Mantra running as Tvamima Oushadhi, etc., never he falls sick. A man by practising the Prati Deva Vrata, is sure to get rid of fears, while a Homa ceremony performed by repeating the Mantras running as Yadindra Munaye, etc., increases the property of the performer. Collyrium applied along the eyelashes by repeating the Mantra running as Bhago No Chitra, etc., is sure to give a better turn, O Rama, to the fortune of the applier, and not the least doubt should be entertained about the success of such a measure. A similar result is obtained by repeating the Mantras running as Indreti Vargam, etc., (6-13).

A man seeking the love of a particular woman, should recite into her ears the Samans running as Paripriya, Hi Vah Kārih, etc., whereby he would surely win her affections. A repetition of the Mantra running as Rathantaram, or the Vamadevyam, increases one's faith in, and knowledge of, the Supreme Brahma, while by daily reciting the verses known as Indramidgathinam, a man is sure to retain in his mind whatever would be spoken to him. By performing a Homa ceremony with the Mantra running as Rathāntaram, a man is sure to be blest with the birth of a son, while repetition of the Manta, running as Mai, Shri, etc., brings more and more good luck every day to its repeater. A man, by daily repeating the eight verses known as he Vairupyas, is sure to become the master of unbounded wealth, whereas by repeating the Sūptāshtakas, a man is enabled to witness the realisation of his heart-felt desires. A man, having subjugated his senses, should worship the cows, each morning, with the verses beginning as Gavyashuna, etc., whereby he would have numerous heads of cattle in his house.

A man by casting oblations of vesselsful (Dronas) of barley, soaked in clarified butter, into the fire, and by repeating the Mantras running as Vāta Avatu, etc., is enabled to cast off all charms and incantations. A man by performing a Homa ceremony with oblations of sesamum and by repeating the Mantras known as Pradeva Dasa followed by Voushtas, becomes an expert in all trades (14-20).

A thousand libations cast into the sacrificial fire with the Mantras, running as Vaskedhāma, etc., grants a victory in war. Effigies of pasted rice should be made of horses, elephants, car-warriors and principal leaders belonging to the enemy's forces, and should be cut with a razor by repeating the mantras running as Abhi Tva Shurananumo, etc., after which the Brahmana engaged to practise the charm, should offer them, in anger, as oblations on the sacrificial fire, mixed with boiling oil. A performance of the rite described above, is sure to grant an easy victory in war. The Mantras known as the Garuda, the Rathāntara, the Vāmadevya and the Vrihadratha should be deemed as undoubtedly the best of sin-expiating Mantras (21-24).

XII

THE RITES AND MANTRAS OF THE ATHARVAN VEDA

PUSHKARA SAID:—

I have done with the Mantras of the Rik and the Sama Vedas, now I shall describe those which appertain to the Atharva Veda and are known as the Atharva rites and Mantras. A man, by performing a Homa ceremony with the Mantras running as Shantatyam Ganam realises God's peace in life, while libations of clarified butter cast with the Mantra, running as Bhaisajyam Ganam, etc., bring about a recovery from all persistent and lingering diseases. A man by pouring libations on the sacrificial fire with the verses known as the Trisaptiyam Ganam, becomes purged off of all sins. Similarly libations of clarified butter offered into the sacrificial fire with the verses known as the Abhaya Ganam, should be deemed as a safeguard against the advent of all evils and dangers, while, O Rama, a man by duly performing a Homa ceremony with the same Mantra, is sure to suffer no defeat in life. A man, by undertaking a Homa with the verses known as the Ayushya Ganam (Life-prolonging Mantras), enjoys an immunity from a premature death, while a Homa performed by repeating the verses known as the Svastyanam Ganam, a man is sure to enjoy a blissful peace in all departments of life (1-4).

A man, by repeating the Mantras running as Shreyascha, etc., is sure to succeed in his practice of Yoga, while a mental recitation of the same Mantra, tends to produce the same result. Defects incidental to one's choosing a bad or a forbidden site for his dwelling-house, are remedied by a Homa, performed by reciting the set of verses known as the Vastospatya Ganam. A man, by casting libations of clarified butter in the sacrificial fire with the set of Atharva verses known as the Roudra Ganam, is sure to make good all defects and shortcomings on his part in life. In a religious ceremony undertaken with a view to confer God's peace on an individual, the number of libations should be increased ten or eighteen times of the number prescribed for the above-said cases, according as the means of the performer of the Homa, or the person on whose behalf the same would be performed, would admit of (5-6).

The manifestations of divine energy respectively known as the Goddess Vaishnavi, etc., as well as the peace-giving rites respectively undertaken in their honour, and known as the Vaishnabi Shanti, the Aindri Shanti, the Roudri Shanti, the Brahmi Shanti, the Vayavya Shanti, the Varuni Shanti, the Kouveri Shanti, the Bhargavi Shanti, the Prajāpatya Shanti, the Tvasta Shanti, the Koumari Shanti, and the peace-giving rites done in honour of the Fire-god (Vanhi Devata), the god of wind (Marut-Gana), as well as those known as the Gāndhari Shanti, the Nairitiki Shanti, the Yāmya Shanti (done in honor of the god of death), the Pārthivi Shanti and the Angirasi Shanti, grant all sort of boons to the performer (7-9).

A repetition of the Mantra running as Yastvam Mrityu, on the occasion of casting libations of clarified butter into the fire, is sure to arrest the death of a person laid up with a fatal disease. A Homa performed with the Mantras running as Suparnastu, etc., grants an immunity from snake-bites, while libations poured on the sacrificial fire with the verses beginning as Indrena Dattam (given by the god Indra), etc., should be deemed as possessed of the virtue of removing all barriers or obstacles standing in one's way. A repetition of the Mantra running as Ime Devi, etc., should be deemed as possessed of a similar peace-giving virtue under all circumstances, while a repetition of the one beginning as Deva Marut, etc., should be held as the grantor of all objects. A recitation of the Mantra running as Yamasya Loka, etc., neutralises the effects of all evil dreams dreamt by a man in the night. A repetition of the Mantra running as Indrascha Pancha Vanija (the god Indra and the five Merchants) brings in a thriving trade. A Homa ceremony performed by repeating the Mantras beginning as Kamo Me Vāji, etc., brings good luck to ladies for whose benefit the same is undertaken. Libations poured on the fire with the Mantra running as Tubhyam Javimān, etc., as well as a repetition of the Mantra beginning as Agne Gobhinna, etc., enlarges one's mind and sharpens one's intellect (10-14).

A man by performing a Homa, and by repeating on the occasion the Mantras running as Dhruvam Dhruvena, etc., becomes the owner of an immoveable estate, while a repetition of the Mantras beginning as Alaktajiva, etc., ensures a prosperous agriculture. A man seeking to improve his social status or fortune, should constantly repeat in his mind the Mantras running as Ahante Bhagna, etc., while a person any way incarcerated, or rotting in jail, would be liberated or set at large by repeating the Mantras, beginning as Ye Me Pāshā, etc., (the fetters that bind me). A man by repeating the Mantras, running as Sapatvāham, etc., and by pouring libations of clarified butter on the fire with the same Mantras, is sure to bring about an utter annihilation of his enemies, while a repetition of the Mantras running as Tamuttamam, etc., is sure to increase one's fame and to give a better turn to one's fortune (15-17).

A repetition of the verses known as the Mrigamati, is sure to give a better turn to the luck of a woman. A repetition of the Mantra, running as Ayante Yoni, etc., (this is thy womb) is sure to impregnate a woman. Similarly a recitation of the Mantra, running as Shivā Shivabhi, etc., brightens the prospect of the repeater. A recitation of the Mantra, beginning as May Vrihaspati protect us (Vrihaspatir No Patu) is the greatest peace-giving rite known, while a repetition of the Mantra, running as Munchāmi Tveti, acts as a safe-guard against all premature death. The man who recites the Mantras known as the Atharva Shiras, is sure to become absolved of all sins (18-21).

I have spoken of several principal rites, to be performed according to the rules of the Atharva Veda. The oblations to be cast into the sacrificial fire, should firstly consist of the tender shoots of the sacrificial trees, while the oblations or libations respectively composed of clarified butter, Vrihi, white mustard, sun-dried rice, sesamum, curd, thickened milk, bunches of green grass, Bel fruits and lotus flowers, should be deemed as the most bliss-giving. O Bhārgava, O thou, foremost of the erudite ones, mustard oil, blood, poison and Rājika, should be cast as oblations into the sacrificial fire, in cases of incantations and spells. The names of the metre and the composers of the verses as well as the purposes for which they are to be used, should be mentioned at each instance (22-25).

XIII

HOW TO WARD OFF THE DREADFUL VISITATIONS OF NATURE

PUSHKARA SAID:—

Now I shall describe the procedure of worshipping the gods, whereby the dreadful visitations of Nature can easily be warded off. A man having bathed and washed himself, should offer the Argha-offering to the god Vishnu, by repeating the three Mantras running as Apohista, etc., while, O thou, twice-born one, the water for washing his feet (Pādyam) should be offered with the three verses beginning as Hiranya Varnā. He should rinse his mouth (Achamanam) with water by repeating the Mantra running as Shanno Apo. While he should sprinkle water over his head with the Mantra, running as Idam Apo. The perfume should be offered by repeating the three Mantras, running as Rathe Akshe, etc., while the cloth should be offered by repeating the Mantra running as Yuvan, etc. Flowers should be offered by repeating the Mantras known as the Pushpavati, while the burning incense-stick should be offered with the Mantras, running as Dhuposhi. The lighted lamps should be waived before the image, and Madhuparkas (small metal cups containing honey should be offered by repeating the Mantras, respectively running as Tejoshi Shukram and Dadhi etc., (1-4).

O thou foremost of human beings, the eight Rics beginning as Hiranya Garbhas, should be used on the occasion of offering boiled rice, cordials, shoes, cushions or carriages, or at the time of blowing chowries unto, or holding an open umbrella over a divine image. The other articles of worship should be offered to the deity by repeating the Savitra Mantras. The verses known as the Pourusha Sukta, should be mentally recited and made use of in connection with a Homa Ceremony. In the absence of any image of idol, the articles of worship, should be offered on the alter or on the full sacrificial pitcher, or on the foreshore of a stream, or on a lotus flower, whereby a votary would win the good graces of the god Vishnu and attain infinite peace on earth.

Then the libations of clarified butter should be poured on the blazing sacrificial fire, lighted on the cushion of sand laid on the well cleansed ground, and spread over with the blades of holy Kusha grass and sprinkled over with consecrated water. Then the self-controlled votary should pour libations on the fire as, "libation to the god Vasudeva:- libation to the Deva, libation to the almighty god (Prabhu) libation to the god who knows no change nor suffers any diminution (Avyaya), libation to the god of fire, libation to the Moon-god, libation to the gods Mitra and Varuna, libation to the god Indra, libation to the gods Indra and Agni." O thou of a generous spirit, then the libation should be offered in honour of the gods, such as the Vishvas, the gods, as the lord of the created beings. O Rama, the subsequent libations should be cast by addressing the goddess Anumati, the god Dhanvantari, the presiding deity of households, the goddess of energy and the fire that created the universe. Then offerings should be made to the above-said deities by addressing their names in the dative case, singular. Similar oblations should be offered to Nerundhi, Dhumrinika, Asvapati, Meghapatni and the goddesses of energy known as Nandini, Subhaga, Sumangala, Bhadrakali, Sthuna, Shri, and Hiranyakeshi, as well as to the Vanaspatis (5-16).

Offerings should be made to the gods of good and evil at the threshold of the temple, to the god of eternal truth (Dhruva) at its centre, to the god of death at the outside, to the god of wealth at the path way, to the god Indra, and his companion deities at the east, to the god of death and his colleagues at the South, to the god Varuna and his comrades at the west, and to the Moon-god and his attendants at the north. Similarly O thou son of Bhrigu, offerings should be made to the god Brahma and his attendant deities at the centre of the temple, and to the spirits that wander in the day light on its floor, ceiling and altar, while in a night-worship, offerings should be made to the spirits that roam about in the dark (17-21).

The offerings should be made to the spirits, night and morning at the outside of the temple, and since oblations should be offered to one's manes, one should take special care to avoid the night fall. A man should offer the first oblation to his deceased father, then to his grandfather, then to his great grandfather, then to his own mother, then to his father's mother, and then to the mother of his grand-father. He should worship the souls of his departed fathers on the tips of the Kushagrass spread out on his right hand side (22-24).

Then oblations should be offered to the crows by repeating the Mantra running as "May the crows who live in the east, west, north west, south and the south west, take and accept this feast, spread out for them.' Then similar oblations should be offered to the dogs, by repeating the Mantra—"Two dogs were born in the family of the sun, one black and one white. I offer them oblations, may they guard my way to the next world." Then oblations should be offered to the cows by repeating the following Mantra." "Accept these oblations, O cows, who are the daughters of the celestial Surabhi and are the mothers of the inmates of the three worlds and who are holy, and given to the good of all, and whose very touches are purifying" (25-27).

Then having offered the above said oblations and doled out alms and charities to the poor, and feasted the assembled guests, a man should perform a Homa ceremony as follows. "Om, libation to Bhu, Om libation to Bhuva. Om, libation to Sva, Om, libation to Bhu, Bhuva and Sva. Om, I pour this libation which is an expiation for sins done to the gods. I offer this libation which is an expiation of sin done to the Petris. Om, I offer this libation which is an atonement for sins done by me. Om, May the sins of mankind be pardoned by the libation I pour on the fire. Om, May the son of sin be pardoned through my offering this libation. Om, I pour on fire this libation of clarified butter which is an atonement for sins wilfully committed by me. Om, I pour on fire this libation to atone for sins unwittingly committed by me. Om, obeisance to the Fire god who is the creator of sacrifices. Om, obeisance to the lord of created beings." I have already dealt with oblations known as the Vaishva 'Deva' Valis and the process of worshipping the god Vishnu (28-29).

XIV

THE ABLUTION FOR EXORCISING THE MALIGNANT SPIRIT VINAYAKA

PUSHKARA SAID:—

Now I shall deal with the rite of ablution which is to be performed for the purpose of exorcising a Vinayaka (a sort of malignant spirit). The spirit Vinayaka was placed by the gods Keshava, Isha and Bramha at the head of the lesser and subordinate gods known as the Ganas, his function being to baffle the ends of men and to frustrate their efforts in general. A man possessed by Vinayaka, sees shaved heads, or fancies himself bathing, or riding on the shoulders of demons or monsters in sleep. He hears the sounds of unseen footsteps closely following his heels in a walk. All his efforts dwindle into nothing at the end, the mind becomes sad, dejected and vacant and loses the power of concentrating itself on any definite subject, and the body withers without any positive ailment. Such a person, if happens to be an unmarried girl, discards all offers of marriage and prefers to continue single, on the contrary a married woman, taken by Vinayaka, refuses the bed of her husband and lives sterile and separate to the end of her life. A disciple under a similar circumstance, becomes averse to his studies and refuses the lessons of his preceptors, whereas in the same predicament a trader foregoes all profits, a cultivator becomes apathetic to his vocation, and monarch neglects the duties of his sovereignty (1-5).

Such a person should take his seat on the sacrificial platform and perform a rite of religious ablution under the auspices of the asterisms known as the Hasta, the Pushya etc., or of those presided over by the Moon-god, Vishnu, or on the occasion of the sun's passing over to a new zodiacal sign, known as the Ashvayuk. He should rub his body with the cake of white mustard and clarified butter, and rub his head with the powders of drugs respectively known as the Sarvoushadhi and Sarvagandha. Then the contents of four pitchers of water containing earth respectively obtained from a stable, an elephant-enclosure, an ant-hill and a confluence of running streams, as well as Rochona, sandal and scented gumresin, and consecrated with the Mantras running as Sahasraksha, and Shatadharam Rishi etc., should be emptied over head. The Mantra which should be recited on the occasion, runs as follows:- "I wash thee with waters obtained from a hundred running streams, hallowed by the touch of the holy sages and the lord of the celestials. May such waters purify thee. May Varuna, the sun-god, Vrihaspati, Indra, the windgod and the seven immortal sages give thee wealth and peace. May the evil fate that sticks to you hair and the ill luck that hangs over your brows and blightens your eyesight, be removed by the efficacy of this consecrated water" (6-12).

Then the preceptor having caught hold of a vessel of Kusha grass, containing mustard oil, should pour out of that on the head of the possessed person, ladlesful of the same substance with his right hand, by repeating the Mantras running as "Libation to Mita, libation to Sanmita, Libation to Shalaka, Libation to Tankata, Libation to Kushmanda, and Libatipn to

Rajaputra", and the term obeisance (Svaha) should be coupled at the end of each of them. Then oblations composed of rawfish, Chitra flowers, cooked fish, boiled rice, radish, cake, curd, thickened milk, Payasa, Modaka and treacle should be offered on a winnow placed at the crossing of four roads, and over a cushion of holy Kusha grass (13-17).

Then the mother of Vinayaka should be invoked and offerings of Durva grass, mustard seeds and flowers should be made to her. Then the final libation should be poured on the sacrificial fire, and the following prayer should be read, "Grant me, O thou, goddess of good luck, the boon of beauty, wealth, progeny and fulfilment of all desires." Then the Brahmanas should be feasted and a pair of cloth should be presented to the ritualist, officiating at the ceremony. A man by worshipping Vinayaka, becomes prosperous, and all his attempts are crowned with success (18-20).

XV

MAHESWARA ABLUTION

PUSHKARA SAID:–

Now I shall deal with the rite of ablution known as the Maheshvara Snanam, which being duly performed, brings victory to the standard of a sovereign, and which was disclosed by the holy sage Ushana to Vali, the king of the demons. The performer of the ceremony should be bathed on the sacrificial platform before sun-rise, and the following Mantra should be read on the occasion. "Om obeisance to the Rudra incarnation of the god and to Vala the (powerful one), whose body is smeared with the ashes of grey colour. Victory and victory thee, O god, trample down all those who would act hostilely to so and so in the quarrel or war that would break out with him. Om, trample down and trample down all comers that are fastly approaching to attack. May the god of white-light, may the god of thousand beams who would burn down the Universe to ashes at the Millemum, accept this worship and protect thy life May the god Shiva, the destroyer of the demon Tripura, and who is possessed of the essence of all the celestial beings, and who, in his Samvarta manifestation, is effulgent like the god of Fire, protect your life. Om obeisance, Likhi, Likhi Likhi," (several editions read Likhi, Lili, Khili). Then having bathed as above indicated, the votary should cast oblations of rice and sesamum into the sacrificial fire, by repeating the above-said Mantra, and bathe the image of the god Shiva with the composition known as the Panchagavya, and worship him thereafter (1-3).

Now I shall describe the other sorts of religious ablutions which grant success to their performers. A bath, after having lubricated the body with clarified butter, tends to increase the duration of life of a man, while by bathing with cowdung, a man becomes a favourite with fortune. Similarly, a bathing, done by rubbing the body with the urine of a cow, makes the bather free from all impieties, while a lubrication of the body with thickened milk before a bath, tends to increase one's mental and physical vigour. By rubbing curd over his body before bath, a man is sure to improve his complexion, while a bath in the washings of the sacred Kusha grass, tends to absolve the bather of all iniquities. A man using the composition of Panchagavya at his bath, becomes possessed of all desirable goods, while a bath in the washings of Asparagus (Shatamuli) or Shringa, respectively ushers in a good fortune, or an unsullied conscience. A bath in the washings of Palasha, Vilva, lotus and Kusha grass, should be deemed as the harbinger of all wished for goods, while the drugs known as the Vacha, the two sorts of Haridras and the Musta, used by a man at his bath, grant him an immunity from the influences of malignant spirits. A bath in the washings of gold, silver or copper, grants longevity and increases the fame, piety and intellectual capacities of the bather. A bath in the washings of gems vouchsafes success in life, while an ablution in water scented with the drugs known as the Sarvagandha (universal perfume), is sure to give a better turn to one's fortune. A daily immersion in a basin of water containing fruits, as well as the use of pulverised Dhatri fruits at the bath, brings in health and beauty. By cleansing the body with powdered sesamum and sun-dried rice at the time of bathing, a man is sure to improve his complexion, while a similar use of the creeper Priyangu, ensures a daily expanding purse. A bath in water saturated with the leaves of Kadamva, Padma and Utpala, brightens one's complexion, while a similar use of the washings of the Vālā plant, increases one's physical strength (4-10).

Of all sorts of bath, the best is that which is done in the washings of the sacred feet of Vishnu. Alone, the bather should pass an entire day in meditation, for the realisation of a single object. He should tie round his wrist a bracelet made of Kustha, Vacha, Shunthi, Conch-shell, or of iron, and by repeating the Shukta, running as Akrandaya, etc., The gift of all sorts of boons is in the hand of the god Hari, and by worshipping him, a man becomes possessed of all wished-for good (11-13).

By bathing the image of the latter deity in a composition of thickened milk and clarified butter, and by duly worshipping it, a man is sure to get rid of all sorts of bilious distempers, while an offering of the five species of Mudga pulse, made to the same deity, should be deemed as an unfailing remedy for all gastric complaints. An immersion of the image of Vishnu in the composition known as the Dvi-Sneha (water and clarified butter), is the best cure for all diseases incidental to a deranged condition of the bodily phlesm. A bath of the above-said emblem in the composition known as the Trirasa, signifies its immersion in a mixture of oil, honey and clarified butter, while an ablution in Dvi-Rasa means its bathing in water and clarified butter only. A Samala Snanam expresses the fact of its being immersed in oil and clarified butter. The composition, known as the Tri Madhuram (the three sweets), consists of honey, juice of sugar-cane and thickened milk, and a bathing of the divine image of Vishnu in it, should be deemed as one the best of peace-giving rites. A mixture composed of oil, clarified butter and sugar-cane-juice, and used for the same purpose as the above, confers, prosperity on the performer of the ceremony. An unguent made of the three white substances (Trishukla) *viz.*, camphor, Ushira, and Sandal, as well as the one composed of Sandal, Agollochum, Camphor, Musk, and Saffron, applied by a votary on the body of an image of Vishnu, enables him to witness the realisation of all his heartfelt objects (14-20).

O thou son of Bhrigu, the three cooling substances usually made use of in a worship of Vishnu, and technically known as the Trisheetas, are the Jati fruits, camphor and sandal. O thou foremost of the race of Bhrigu, articles of five different colours such as e yellow, the grey, the white, the black and the red, are usually employed in the service of the above-said deity. The three white articles are the Utpala, the lotus and the Jati flowers. Saffron, the red lotus, and the red Utpala flowers from the three red and so on. By worshipping the so with lighted lamps and burning incense-sticks, an man is enabled to enjoy god's peace in life. The Brahmanas should perform a Homa ceremony in such a connection, in a quadrilateral fire-hole, and respectively pour a hundred thousand, or a million libations of barley, sesamum, paddy and clarified butter on the sacrificial fire, and thereafter worship the planets with the Gayatri Mantra, whereby the greatest bliss would be brought about (21-24).

XVI

THE MANTRAS FOR CONSECRATING THE ROYAL UMBRELLA

PUSHKARA SAID:—

Now I shall narrate the Mantras with which the royal umbrella should be consecrated, and victory is sure to follow from worshipping it with them. "May thy splendour and majesty grow from more to more every day, with the dynamics of truth which is the essence of the god Brahma, and the light and energy that burns within the suns and moons, and the force that moves in the spirit of the mighty Water god. May thy paramount authority be consolidated more and more every day, O thou the Royal Umbrella, the source, the centre of all nobleness and lofty aspirations. May the king repose in health and victory beneath thy blissful shade, as the earth rests in bliss under the shadow of a pregnant rain-cloud. O thou grey-coloured emblem of low and order, O thou whose lustre resembles the mellow bean of a snow-ball or autumn-moon, O thou who art born of the race of Gandharvas, mayst thou never defile the race of our sovereigns. Increase in majesty and splendour, O thou the Royal horse, with the undying truth which is the self of Brahma, with the immortal energy that burns in the sun and moon and fire, with the pieties and penances that have made their sanctuaries in the hearts of the holy sages, with the annihilation of animal propensities that characterises Rudra, and with the force that sets the winds in motion. Recollect thy royal birth, O thou horse, the metamorphised son of a sovereign, and the gem Koustabha that was churned out of the primeval ocean with thy honoured self. The sin that appertaineth to a killer of a Brahmana, the sin that is incidental to a patricide or matricide, the sin that sticketh to the cursed throat of a making a false claim to a plot of ground, the sin that dogs the fugitive foot-steps of a cowardly Kshatriya, showing his back to his enemies in battle, may never lie on your lofty head, and may they fly before thy bold and courageous front. In road, in battle, may you never belie your noble origin and descent, and may you kill the enemies of your royal master in battle, and live happily with him in his service" (1-9).

"I lay myself at thy feet, O thou lord of the celestial birds, O thou Guruthmana of mighty opinions, O thou son of Vinata who sittest perched on the standard of Narayana, and movest like a banner before the armed hosts of the lord of the celestials. Lead me to new victories every day, O thou whose movements are swifter than those of the wind. O thou immense-bodied quaffer of divine ambrosia who destroyed the serpents and the enemies of god-head in battle, and didst steal away the bowl of nectar for the benefit of the universe. Fill in the ranks of any battled legions, O thou god of matchless prowess. Never leave my lines, O thou invincible spirit of immense agility. Protect me and my soldiers, clad in mailed armours, O thou whom the supreme Vishnu appointed to shield the person of the celestial king, and burn the ranks of my hostile forces" (10-13).

The eight elephants known as, Kumuda, Airavata, Padma Pushpadanta, Vamana, Supritaka, Anjana and Nila, are of divine origin. Their sons and sons' sons such as, Bhadra, Manda, Mriga, etc., multiplied themselves in the forests of the earth. "O you royal elephants, recollect your divine progenitors and the celestial blood that courses in your veins. May the Vasus, the Rudras, the Adityas, and the Maruts protect you all. O thou king of the elephants, protect thy sovereign master and rigidly discharge the obligation he has laid thee under. May the king of the gods riding on his mighty Airavata (elephant), follow thee in battle and guard thy rear. Win victory in battle and enjoy perpetual health. May you wax as hot in battle as thy divine cohort Airavata. May you acquire beauty from the moon-god, strength from Vishnu, energy from the sun, speed from the god of wind, steadiness from mountains, victory from Rudra, and fame from the god Purandara. May the divine elephants with their respective celestial riders, protect thee in battle. May the Ashvinis, together with the Maruts, the Gandharvas, the Vasus, the Rudras, the immortal sages, the wind, and the moon-god protect thee in all the quarters of the globe. May the Nagas, the Kinnaras, the Gandharvas, the Yakshas, the ghosts, the planets, the Pramathas, the presiding deities of malignant spirits, and the Matricas, the god Indra, the Commander-in-Chief of the heavenly forces, and the god Varuna strengthen thy limbs with their respective essences, and burn down to ashes the battled hosts led by the enemy of this victory-seeking monarch" (14-22).

"Recollect the debt you owe to thy sovereign, O streamer, float in victory and gladness to-day, as thou didst flutter in battles which led to the falls of Kalanemi, Tripura, Hiranya-Kashipu, and other demons. May the ornaments with which the enemy's standard has been decorated, fall to the ground, struck by thy unbearable energy. May the enemies of the king be totally annihilated, affected by thy blue, and white, colours. May pestilence and virulent epidemics break out in the ranks of the enemy's forces, and may Putana, Revati, Lekha, Kālarātri and other monstresses follow in their wake and devour them all" (34-28).

"O sword, the god Sharva created thee of yore in the great religious sacrifice known as the Mahayajna, and out of the essence of the universe. The eight appellations by which thou art known are, (1) Krishna, (2) Shrigarbha, (3) Vijaya, (4) Dharmapala, (5) Asi,

(6) Khadga, (7) Tikshna Dhara and (8) Durasada. O thou destroyer of the evil disposed, O thou, who dost neutralise the effects of bad dreams, O thou, whose colour resembles the hue of a blue lotus, these are the eight epithets given to thee by the god Shambhu of yore. Remember when thou wert manifest in the shape of the god Nandaka, O thou, those entire length exceeds the measure of thirty fingers (Nistrinsha). Thy nativity is marked by the asterism Krittika, the god Maheshvar is thy preceptor, thy body is made of gold, and the god Janardana is the presiding deity of thy existence. Protect the king, O Sword, with all his household and subject-people and army. Out of thee, the universe has evolved into its present shape. I make obeisance to thee, O thou sinless one, O thou who dost help thy votaries to bring a battle to a glorious and happy termination. O thou, who dost protect the soldiers as a mailed coat, save my honour, army and prestige to-day, I am a fit object of thy pity" (29-34).

"O thou trumpet, whose dreadful flourishes strike terror into the hearts of one's enemies, dost thou add to the signal glory of the royal arms. As the mighty tuskers rejoice at the deep rumbling sound of a rain-could, so may the thrilling peals of thy soul-stirring notes fill our men with joy, animation and a maddening thirst for martial glory. As a timid and forlorn wife trembles in her lonely bed, at the clap of thunder in a dark and drizzling night, so may our hostile army tremble at thy fatal or death-dealing note" (35-37).

Each year, the royal arms and insignias should be worshipped by repeating the above-said Mantras, which should be used as well on the occasion of a royal inauguration by the king's astrologer. Similarly, the image of the god Vishnu should be consecrated with the offerings of blankets, etc., dedicated to his divine use (38).

XVII

THE INCANTATION OF VISHNU PANJARAM

PUSHKARA SAID:—

O thou foremost of the twice-born ones, the god Brahma employed the Mantra known as the Vishnu Panjaram, for the protection of the god Shankara, bent on killing the demon Tripura. Again the same Mantra was used for a similar purpose by Vrihaspati, in connection with Indra's setting out on a war against the demon Vala, in which the later was slain. Now I shall describe the real nature of the incantation to be practised on the occasion, and the Mantras that are to be used in connection with the same (1-3).

The god Vishnu, wielding a discus in his hand, should be contemplated as occupying the eastern portion of the circle of incantation (Mantra Chakra), the mace-wielding Hari as situated as its south, the god Vishnu holding a bow in his hand, as occupying the western part of the circle round the warrior, the god Janardana with a sword in his hand in the north, the god Hrishikesha at the angular points of the circle, and the god Janardana as occupying their intervening spaces. Similarly he should contemplate the god Vishnu, manifest in the shape of Kroda, as filling in the ground he stands upon, and the god Nrisinha as pervading the span of heaven above his head. Then the following Mantra should be repeated:- The discus Sudrashanam, burning with the effulgence of the mid-day-sun, is revolving over my head. May its scorching and unbearable light, kill the ghosts and monsters that are conspiring to bring about my destruction. May the mace of the god, resplendent as the sun of the millennim, or burning with the glow of living fire, kill the demons, monstersy, Pishachas and Dakinis that are concocting evils for my ruin. May the bow of the god Vasudeva, cast ruin and confusion broadcast among the ranks of my enemies, and men, and Kushmandas and Pretas and fiendish creatures that are brewing mischief for my fall. May the sworn brotherhood of demons be defeated, frustrated and dispersed by the moon-shine-lustre of the irrresistible sword of Vishnu, as serpents are routed by the mighty presence of the invincible Guruthmana. May all the Kushmandas, Yakshas, Daityas, Nishacharas, Pretas, Vinayakas, wicked men, lions, tigers, serpents and birds of prey, change their vicious nature, and be amiably disposed towards me. May all those who are practising dreadful incantations to obliterate my memory, or to deaden my intellectual faculties in general, as well as the Kushmandas who are attempting to deprive me of my comforts and enjoyment, or to screen my signs of auspicious omen, perish root and branch, struck by the almighty discus of Vishnu. May my body, mind and senses harmoniously act in healthy unison, through the favour of the ever-kind Vasudeva" (4-13).

"The god Hari is guarding me both at the back and the front. The god Hari is protecting me at the north and the south. Thou art the infinite, worship-

ful, changeless god. The man who bows down to
thee, knows no affliction. The god Keshava is indentical
with the supreme Brahma. The universe is the embodied
self of the god Hari. I, with a whole heart,
sing the name of the god. May my three sorts of sin
be pardoned" (14-15).

XVIII

THE TWO DIVISION OF THE VEDIC MANTRAS

PUSHKARA SAID:—

The Mantras a contained in the Rik, Atharva,
Saman and Yajur Vedas number hundred thousands
in all. They were divided into two main branches,
viz., Ashvalayana, and Voudhayana. The ten thousand
Mantras contain two thousand Brahmanas. The
holy sages Dvaipayana, etc., remembered the Rikveda.
The Yajurveda contains one thousand nine hundred
and ninty-nine Mantras. The ten thousand Brahmanas
are divided into eighty six branches, such as the
Kanva, Madhyandini, Kathi, and Madhyakati, etc. The
Shakhas (branches) known as the Maitriyani, Taittriya,
Vaishampayanika, etc., belong to the Yajurveda. The
first Shakha, belonging to the Sama Veda, is called
the Kouthumi, the second is known as the tharvanayani,
and the four Ganas are the Aranyakas belonging to
it. The Ukthas and the Mantras such as the four
Uhas number nine thousand in all. The Brahma Sankatas
number hundred and four in all, out of which twenty-five
appertain to the Sama Veda (1-8).

The sages, such as Shounaka, Pippalada, Munchakesha,
Sumanta, Javali, etc., were the first rhapso-

dists who sang the verses of the Atharva Veda. The holy Vyasa, an incarnation of the Supreme Brahma, divided the Vedas into different groups or Shakhas, each containing ten thousand and six hundred Mantras and a hundred Upanishads. The god Vishnu, manifest in the shape of the holy Vyasa, also composed the books known as the Puranas and the Itihasas. The six sages such as Suta, Lomaharsana, Sumati, Agni-Varcha, Mitraya, Shanshapayana, Kritavrata ad Savarni, having received the Puranas from the holy Vyasa, became his disciples. The sages, such as Sanshapayana, etc., made Sanhitas of the eighteen Puranas, such as the Brahma, etc. The god Hari who is beyond all illusion, and of whom has evolved out this illusory universe, and who though shapeless, sometimes assumes a definite form, and who is the fountain source of all knowledge, is the pervading spirit of the present work (Agni Puranam). A man by worshipping and singing hymns in praise of the god (Vishnu), is enabled to enjoy all the creature comforts in this life, and to work out his salvation in the next (9-17).

The Almighty, ever victorious Vishnu, is manifest in the fire and in the sun. As fire, he serves as the mouth of the gods, by receiving the libation offered in the course of a sacrifice. The god (Vishnu), as manifest in the shape of the religious sacrifice, forms the theme of the Vedas and the Puranas. The present work (Agni Puranam) is the best of all shapes that had ever been assumed by the infinite Vishnu. The god Janardana is the author and hearer of the present Agni Puranam. Therefore, the present work is full of the essence of all the Vedas, and ranks supreme among its sister compositions. The Agni Puranam is replete with all knowledge worth acquiring, is holiest of the holies, and is great with the infinite greatness of the god Hari. One in quest of wisdom, should read and hear the verses of the present work recited, whereby he will gain proficiency in learning, since it (Agni Puranam) is but another manifestation of the god Hari running through all as universal soul. The seekers of beauty, wealth, kingdom, virtue, fame, learning, cow, village and attributes of good fortune in general, are sure to attain their respective objects of solicitation by a single perusal of the present work. The Agni Puranam grants salvation to those earnestly strive for liberation of their souls, engaged whereas by going through it, the worst sinners may purge off the sins that lie thick on their souls (18-22).

XIX

THE MANTRAS WHICH GRANT ALL CREATURE COMFORTS

SAID THE GOD OF FIRE:—

Now listen to me discoursing on the congery of Mantras, a knowledge whereof grants to their respective votaries enjoyment of all the creature comforts in this life, and salvation in the next. O thou twice-born one, the Mala-Mantras consist of more than twenty letters. The Vijas in order to be classed as Arvak-Mantras, must consist of more than ten letters. The Arvak-Mantras constantly repeated, bear fruits at their old age, *i.e.*, they grant salvation to their reciters at the lapse of the full period for which they are enjoined to be repeated. The Vija-Mantras which generally consist of less than ten letters, fructify at the middle of their enjoined time, *i.e.*, at their youth. The Mantras which consist of more than five and less than ten letters, may bear fruit at any time of their ordained period for repetition (1-3).

The Mantras are usually reckoned as belonging to masculine, feiminine, or to neuter sex. The feminine Mantras invariably end with the term Svaha, the name of the wife of the Fire-god, while those that are of the neuter sex, end with term Namas (obeisance), the rest being held as masculine. The Mantras of the male sex, should be used in charms, or in those mystic practices which tend to distract the minds of one's enemies. The feminine Mantras should be made use of in acts of little moment, or in those which are undertaken with the sole object of bringing sound health on them on whose behalf they are practised. The Mantras which are reckoned as belonging to the female sex, should be used in al other sorts of charms. The Mantras are again grouped under the two more broader sub-divisions of Soumya, (soothing), and Agneya (fiery). The Vijas known as the Tara, should be appended to both the Soumya, and the Agneya-Mantras. The Agney-Mantras usually end with a Tara-Vija. The Soumya-, or the Agneya-, Mantras, should be used in an act which is of a nature quite in conformity with the meaning of either of them. An Agneya Mantra may be converted into a Soumya one, by adding the term Fut (obeisance) to its end (4-7).

A Mantra which is asleep, or has been just roused out of its state of slumber, does not bear fruit, though ardently repeated in rapid succession, and for ages and ages together. The sleeping state of a Mantra should be ascertained from the rapid and fluttered emission of breath through both the nostrils, while its waking should be judged from the calm and uniform passing of the wind through the left. An Agneya-Mantra may be converted into one of the Soumya class, by repeating its component letters in an inverse order. The state of waking of both these Mantras, should be carefully ascertained, and letters or Vijas which are presided over by baneful planets and asterisms, should be scrupulously excluded there from. In acts of charm, practised for the acquisition of a kingdom, or for the benefit of an individual, the vowel letters which are inimical to the component letters of his name, should be first arranged in due order. The Mantras are to be ascertained from computations made on the table on which the Gopal-Mantras are calculated, or by means of a Nakshatra Chakra. The letters of the alphabet from A to AS [excepting the two Ris and the two Lis], should be arranged under the different asterisms from Ashvini to Rohini, or the different chambers of the former diagram should be marked as the Siddha [successful, such as the ninth, the first and the fifth chamber], Sadhya [successful in time, such as the sixth, the tenth and the second chamber], the Susiddha [extremely successful, such as the third, the seventh and the eleventh chamber], and the Ari [Hostile, such as the fourth, the eighth, and the twelfth chamber], and the character of each Mantra in relation to the name of the individual to whom it should be imparted, should be calculated therefrom. A man, by simply repeating a siddha-Mantra, attains salvation, while a Sadhya-Mantra requires the performance of the rites of Homa and worship, to be at all fruitful. A mere contemplation of a Susiddha-Mantra, is enough for the salvation [attainment of absolute knowledge] of its votary. A repetition of a hostile Mantra, is sure to lead its votaries to the grave. A Mantra, full of forbidden or baneful letters of the alphabet, should be carefully avoided (8-15).

A man, having been duly initiated into the mysteries of a Tantric worship, and having been duly blest with the rite of final Ablution (Abhisheka) by his religious preceptor, should repeat the Mantras, obtained from him. A Brahmana who is scrupulously truthful, pure, intelligent, possessed of god-like fortitude, given to Japa and meditation, fully conversant with the books of Scripture, practises penances, and is capable of elevating or chastening his disciple, should be acknowledged as a Guru. A disciple, on the other hand, should live on a purely vegetable or Havishya diet, cultivate liberal sentiments, never allow his mind to be ruffled by any consideration of the world, practise self-control and live the highest intellectual life possible, and should be a man always eager to learn fresh spiritual laws, heartily devoted to the service of his Guru, whom he should help with money, if necessary. A Guru, having imparted a Mantra to hi disciple, should repeat it ten thousand times for its perfect fruition (16-19).

A disciple stand in the relation of a son to his Guru. A Mantra heard at random, or obtained by force or stratagem from a Guru, or any Mantra found written on a leaf, or imparted in the form of a gatha (a peculiar meter of ballad poetry), should be looked upon as absolutely barren. The man who had nearly perfected a Mantra with rites of Homa and worship in a previous existence, is sure to work out his salvation in his next or succeeding birth, with a little labour upon the same (20-20).

There is nothing, which a person who has perfected even a single Mantra, is not capable of doing, not to speak of the man who has spent his life in perfecting many. Such a man is no less than the god Shiva himself. A Mantra consisting of a single Mantra, bears fruit after being repeated a million times. A Mantra consisting of a good many number of letters, should not be repeated so many times, while a Mantra consisting of letter, numbering twice or three as much as its Vija-Mantras, should be repeated in the way of a Rosary-Mantra. A Mantra should be repeated hundred and eight, or a thousand, times, where no definite number of repetition would be mentioned and in all cases, libations of clarified butter numbering a tenth part of the number of Mantras repeated, should be poured on the sacrificial fire. Libations, should consist of clarified butter alone, where no particular substance should be enjoyed in that behalf. A man, incapable of performing the rite of necessary Homa, should further repeat a tenth part of the number of the Mula-Mantra, duly evoked, is pleased with the final ceremony of Homa, worship and meditation, and grants the wished-for boon to the votary (23-27).

A Mantra repeated in a small voice, should be deemed as ten more meritorious than the one repeated in a loud tone, whereas the one repeated in a voice scarcely audible, but which is only judged from the constant movements of the tongue, is hundred times more efficacious than the latter, while a mental repetition of the Mantra, should be deemed as a thousand times more fruitful than that. A votary should repeat the Mantra, sacred to his tutelary god, with his face turned either to the north or to the east. All Mantras should be repeated by prefixing the Pranava Mantras to them. The votary should be a man, not given to much talk, nor addicted to unholy drink and unclean diet. With his tongue fully controlled, and appetites fully subjugated, he should take his seat, at the lonely shore of a lake or a river, or amidst the sanctified solitude of a temple or open field, and there repeat his Mantras, without making any distinction between the person of his Guru and that of his tutelary god. For the absolute fruition of the Mantra, the votary should live on a Havishya diet, or take wheat-cakes soaked in milk, on the day of its repetition. The regent of the Mantra should be worshipped under the auspices of the eighth or the fourteenth day of the moon's wane, or on the occasion of a solar or a luner eclipse (28-32).

The gods, such as, Dasra, Yama, the fire-god the god of fate, the moon, the Rudras, the regent of the planet Jupiter, the heavenly serpents, the Pitris, Vaga, Aryaman, the sun, Tvasta, the Maruts, Indra, the fire-god, the Mitras and Indra, Niriti, the water-god, the Vishvadevas, Hrisikesha, the winds, the god of ocean, Ajaikapad, Ahirvadna, Pusha, the Ashvins, the Adi-devatas, the fire-god and Asra, Uma, Nighna, the Nagas, the moon-god, the sun, the Matris, Durga, the guardian deities of the different quarters of the sky, Krishna, Vaivasvata, and Shiva, should be deemed as the presiding deities of the different days of a lunar month, whereas the days of the week should be respectively held sacred to the deities such as Hara, Durga, Guru, Vishnu, Brahma, Lakshmi and Dhanesvara (33-37).

Now I shall deal with the rite of Lipinyasa, or the mystic act of contemplating the different parts of the body, as permeated with the essence of the divinities represented by each letter of the alphabet (Matrika Varnas). The letters constituting the five groups or Vargas of Consonants, [such as the Ka Varga, the Cha Varga, the Ta Varga, the Tha Varga, and the Pa Varga], should be contemplated as permeating in couples, the region of the scalp, of the eyes, of the ears, of the nose, of the cheeks, of the lips, of the teeth, of the head, of the mouth, of the back, of the sides, and the region of the umbilicus, and so on, with the energy of their symbolised divinities. The region of the heart should be made permeated with the essence of the letters such as Ya, etc., which would be driven deep into the seven cardinal principles of life, such as the serum, the blood, the flesh, the fat, the bone, the marrow and the semen. The regent of the letters are Srikantha, Ananta, Sukshma, Trimurti, Amarishvara, Agnisha, Bhavabhuti, Tithisha, Sthanuka, Hara, Dandisha, Bhoutika, Sadyojata, Anugrahishvara, Akrura, and Mahasena (38-41).

Then the names of the different manifestations of Rudra, such as, Krodhisha, Chanda, Panchantaka, Shivottama, Rudra, Kurma, Trinetra, Chaturanana, Ajesha, Sarva, Somesha, Langali, Daraka, Ardhanarishvara, Umakanta, Ashadi, Dandi, Atri, Mina, Mesha, Lohita, Sikhi, Chhagalanda, Dviranda Mahakala, Vali, Bhujanga, Pinaki, Khadgi, Vaka, Shveta, Bhrigu, Lagudisha, Aksha and Samvartaka, should be contemplated as written in fire inside the different parts of the body, each followed by the term Namas (42-47).

The votary should locate the Anga-Mantras, in the different parts of his body, with the principle ones. The Anga-Mantras, such as, the Namas, the Svaha, etc., should be located in the following order, *i.e.*, the term Namas should be contemplated as situated at the region of the heart, the term Svaha at the tuft of hair on the crown, the Mantra Hrum, as protecting the body of the votary as an armour, the Mantra Voushat, as occupying the region of the eyes, and the Mantra Fut as a weapon in the hand of the votary. Oblations consisting of sesamum seeds, should be cast into the sacrificial fire, in honour of the goddess of learning, who should be contemplated as holding a rosary and a pitcher in her two right hands, and a book and a lotus in her two left. The goddess, thus worshipped, fills her votary with the fire of poesy. The rite in question, should be performed at the beginning of a ceremony, for the fructification of the object of its undertaking. The Mantras becomes spotless when preceded by such a rite of Nyasa (48-51).

XX

THE MANTRAS DESTROYING THE BANEFUL INFLUENCES OF MALIGNANT STARS

SAID THE GOD FIRE:—

Now I shall narrate to you the Mantras, that tend to destroy the baneful influences, cast down by malignant planets. Five different types of insanity have been noticed in actual practice, which are originated by excessive joy, by a strong but unfulfilled desire, by unclean food, or by a diet composed of substances that are incompatible to one another, or by the wrath of gods and preceptors, or are ushered in through a deranged state of all the three vital humours, as well as the one, that is due to an external cause, such as a blow, or a hurt (1-2).

The gods, terrified at the wrath of Rudra, disguised themselves in the shape of the planets (Grahas), who possess a man, found alone, and loitering about the solitary shores of a lake, stream, or a river, or at the confluence of streams, or treading his way along the solitary brow of a hill, or taking his rambles in a lonely garden, or walking over a bridge, or crossing a moor or a field, the monotony of which is broken by the presence of a single, haunted tree, or staying at a lonely or a deserted house. The conditions under which a woman is likely to be possessed by one of such malignant planets, are, that she would be in the family way, or sleeping under the naked sky, or in an open room, with dishevelled hairs, and disarranged garments, or that she would be a girl, about to be converted into a woman, or a maiden in her flow, bathing in utter nudity after the period of her uncleanness (3-5).

The evil influence of a malignant planet on a person, is marked by vicissitudes of fortune, loss of prestige, and the hostile conduct of his former friends. Such a man does not hesitate to impugn the dignity of his elders, and superiors, outstrips the boundary of decency or decorum, and acts in direct contravention of the rules of his religion and society. He is furious, and frantically brushes his hairs with both the hands, listens to the evil counsel of lonely mountain-summits, and yields to the temptation of ending his life, by a leap therefrom. Fits of weeping are followed by paroxysms of weird laughter. The victim looks agitated, tosses his head in agony, while his blood shot-eyes, mark the highly congested state of the brain. All appetite vanishes, or at times the patient complains of thirst and hunger, or of a colic pain in the abdomen, and a burning sensation of the skin. At times, he is compassionate, or thinks himself a god, and asks for offerings, of whomsoever he comes across.

A woman, in such a predicament, becomes excessively fond of flowers, perfumes and articles of luxury in general, and takes constant ablutions. She is fond of the company of the stronger sex, knows no satiety, and exhibits all the symptoms, peculiar to Nymphomania. The Mantras sacred to the celestial discus (Sudarshanam), to the all pervading Vitapanasa, to the goddess Chandi, or to the redoubtable Narsinha, are possessed of the virtue of neutralising the effects of all active poison, or of exorcising the baneful influences of malignant spirits and planets. The regent of the sun, should be contemplated, as a deity fond of Prishni, Asafoetida, Vacha, and Shirisha flowers, and wielding a noose, a mace, a khattanga, a lotus, a rosary, a human skull, and a spear in his hands. The god should be contemplated, as possessed of four faces, and seated on a full-blown lotus flower, that waves on the blue etherial constituent of the solar disc. The god should be worshipped with his companion Adityas, and offerings should be made to him, as soon as the solar disc would be visible above the horizon at dawn (6-12).

The regent of the planet Venus, should be contemplated as a Brahmana, seated before a reservoir of sacrificial fire, sunk into the ground, and attended by his Vijas, Shvasa, Visha, Agni, etc. The offerings, should be made to the regions of the Bhu, Bhuva, Sva, etc., in connection with the worship of the sun-god, and to the energy of light (Jvalini) as well, which serves as a mace to that deity. The god Arun, the precursor of the glow of day, should be contemplated as a god of red colour, clad in vermil-tinted garments, and seated on a full-blown lotus flower, accompanied by the god Vishvaka, and the goddess of light. The regent of the moon, should be contemplated as a god, compassionately disposed, extremely beautiful in person, richly embellished with ornaments, and attended upon by the god Vishvaka, and the goddess of glow (Dyuti). The god, should be imagined, as attended upon by a number of celestial youths of matchless beauty, all wielding lotus flowers in their hands, and engaged in blessing the world with divine benediction The regent of the planet Mars, should be contemplated as possessed of a vermil-red complexion, and clad in a garb of lightning. The regent of the planet Mercury, should be contemplated as possessed of a white complexion (*sic*.), while those of the regents of the Jupiter and the Venus, should be respectively deemed as yellow and white. The regent of the planet Saturn, is possessed of a dark blue (Krishna) complexion while those of the nodes, both ascending and descending, are like charcoal and smoke respectively. Their left hands, should be contemplated as placed on their respective left thighs, while the right hands, should be imagined as bent in, a posture which says, "Dread not" (13-16).

The priest should purify the palms of his hands, by psychically locating therein, the effulgent energy of the Astra Mantra, and project, by an act of Nyasa, into the regions of his eyes and thumb-tips, the energy of the Hrid Mantra coupled with the Vijas, the first letters of their respective names. He should contemplate his own Self, as fully permeated with the essence of the latter Mantras. Then having performed the rite of Nyasa, with the three principal and the Anga Mantras, he should wash the vessel of divine service, by repeating the Astra Mantra, and by pouring down water with a repetition of the principal ones. The lowers, sun-dried rice, sandal paste, Durva-grass, and the Argha offering, should be consecrated with the same Mantra. Then he should sprinkle the consecrated water over his own body, and purify therewith the articles of worship, spicad before him. Then having meditated upon the self of the absolute, infinite, and perfect purity which is the underlying substratum of infinite and unchangeable felicity as well, he should contemplate the cushion of the god (Pitha), as formed of the essence of the Hrid Mantra,- the cushion, spread out in the form of a full-blown lotus flower, its petals pointing towards the eight cardinal and angular points of the sky, offering seats to the eight companion goddesses of energy (17-21).

The eight goddesses should be worshipped with the Vija Mantras, sacred to each of them, as follows:—Vam, obeisance to the goddess of light, Veem, obeisance to the goddess of latent energy, Vum, obeisance to the goddess of victory, Voum, obeisance to the solar energy, that is blissful to the world, Vem, obeisance to the divine energy of the sun, Vaim, obeisance to the Vimala energy, Vom, obeisance to the electric flash that emits from the sword-stroke of the sun-god, Voum, obeisance to the solar energy that pervades all space, Vam, obeisance to the throne of the sun-god, and Vah, obeisance to the sun himself. The priest, an adept in practising penances, should then invoke the sun-god, and worship him with a repetition of the Hrid Mantra, and with the six essential articles (Sadanga) of worship, such as the water for washing the feet, and rinsing the mouth, etc.

The Hrid, sacred to the sun-god, consists of a concourse of celestial spirits, such as the two Khakaras, the two Chandas, the spirit Jaradvahu, the goddess Mansa-Dirgha, etc., and grants all boons to the votary, when duly worshipped. Similarly the Hrids, respectively sacred to the god of fire, the Maruts, and the lord of the Rakshas, should be worshipped at the angular points of the Mandala, with the Mantras sacred to each of them. The planets, such as the Moon, the Mercury, the Jupiter, and the Venus, should be worshipped at the four cardinal points of the Mandala. The drags known as the Patha, Pathya, Vacha, Shigru, Sindhu, and Vyosha, should be separately pasted with the urine of a goat, and the compound thus prepared, should be used either as a snuff or a collyrium, whereby the evil influences of malignant planets would be removed. Ordinary cow-butter, boiled with the thickened milk of a she-goat, should be deemed as possessed of a similar efficacy. A decoction composed of the drugs, known as the Vrischik, Ali, Phali, Kustha, salts and Sharngakam, would prove beneficial to a person suffering from that peculiar type of Hysteria, which is ascribed to the evil influence, exerted by a malignant planet. 1 A decoction composed of the expressed juice of Vidari, Kusha, and Ikshu, as well as clarified butter boiled with Yastika and the essence of Drona, and Kushmanda, or clarified butter mixed with the Panchagavya, may be given with advantage to patient, suffering from a similar kind of mental aberration (22-29).

Now, hear me discourse on the treatment to be adapted is a case of fever, due to such a cause as above indicated. The Gyatri Mantra, sacred to the spirit of fever, and which runs as "Om, let us know the nature of the deity, whose strength reduces all beings to ashes. Let us meditate on the divine self of that single-tusked god. May fever lead cur mind to dwell on that," should be devoutly recited for its subsidence.

In the alternative, a paste composed of Krishna, Ushan, Nisha, Rasna, oil pressed out of grapes, and treacle, should be applied at intervals, on the tongue of the patient. A case of such fever, accompanied by cough and other bronchial troubles, would yield to a paste, composed of Bhargi, Yasthi, honey, and clarified butter, or Patha, Ticta, Kana, Bhargi and honey, administered as in the preceding case. A paste, composed of Dhatri, Vishva, Sita, Krishna, Musta, Kharjura, Magadhi, and honey, and taken as above, would prove beneficial to such symptoms, as hiccough, etc., that are developed in the course of the disease. In the alternative, a paste composed of any of the three substances, enumerated in the preceding line, should be licked with honey, by a man, suffering from a swellings of the limbs, in the course of such fever. A person, afflicted with jaundice which invariably marks the sequel to such a malady, should be treated with a decoction, composed of the expressed juice of Jiva, Manduki, Nisha, and Dhatri, while any sort of cough, would prove amenable to a powder, composed of Vyosha, Padmaka, Triphala, Vidanga, Devadaru, Rasna, common treacle, mixed in equal proportions (30-38).

XXI

THE PRINCIPAL MANTRAS SACRED TO THE LORD OF HEAVEN

SAID THE GOD OF FIRE:-

The principal Mantra sacred to the lord of heaven, consists of the Vijas known as the Vak, Karma, etc., and end with the one known as the Huta. The Mantra should be repeated a hundred thousand times, whereby the intellect of the repeater is sure to be expanded. The Hrid Mantra sacred to the god Indra, consists of Vijas, known as the Atri, Agni, Vama, Akshi and Vindu. The god should be contemplated as possessed of a yellow complexion, and wielding a thunderbolt and a lotus flowers in his hands. Ten thousand libations of clarified butter, containing seeds of sesamum, should be poured on the sacred fire in honour of the god, and his image should be bathed with the Panchagavya, whereby a king, dispossessed of his kingdom, would recover its lost possession, or a man not blest with any children, would be the founder of a happy family. The Sakti Mantra, consisting of Dosha,

Agni, and Danda Vijas, should be repeated on the eighth and the fourteenth day of a lunar month, with a view to secure the salvation of one's own soul. The goddess should be contemplated as wielding a discus, a noose, and a mace in her three hands, the fourth being imagined as held in the attitude of giving encouragement, or saying benediction. The worship should be concluded with a rite of Homa, in course of which ten thousand libations of clarified butter, should be poured on the sacrificial fire, whereby the votary would be rewarded with a poetic genius and the birth of an heir (1-6).

"Om, Hrim, Om Obeisance to the god of desire who is good to all sentient creatures, and who charms the hearts of all, and is effulgent as the living fire. Bring, O Bring the hearts of all under my control, Om."

Having duly repeated the above said Mantra, a man would acquire ascendency over the things and inmates of the whole universe.

"Om, Hrim, O thou Chamunda, burn and burn, cook and cook such and such a person, and make his mind subservient to that of my own, Tha, Tha."

The above Mantra sacred to the goddess Chamunda, should be deemed as the best of charms. A wife, should wash her Vagina with the expressed juice of the drugs known as the Triphala, whereby she would be able to win her husband's affections for good. Similarly a wife should apply over her private parts, a paste composed of Ashvagandha, barley, turmeric, camphor, Pippali, the eight sorts of grain known as the Ashtadhanya, Vrihati, and twenty black pepper, who would thereby retain the affections of her husband to the last day of her life. A paste composed of powdered Kathira roots and honey, should be deemed as possessed of the same virtue, and should be used by a woman in the way mentioned in the preceding line. A liniment composed of camphor, Magadhi, honey and the expressed juice of the Kapitthaka, should be used both by the husband and the wife with a view to increase their loving and affectionate regard for each other. A liniment composed of sugar and the expressed juice of Kadamva, and applied along the passage of child birth by a woman, would make her a doted favourite with her husband. A compound, consisting of powdered Sahadevi, Mahalakshmi, Putrajiva, and Kritanjali should be strewn over the head of a person for the same end (7-12).

A prastha measure of the decoction of Triphala and sandal wood, and two kudava weights of Bhringa, Hemrasa and Dosha, and an equal weight of honey, Chunchaka, and turmeric, should be boiled with clarified butter and dried in the shade. The powder thus prepared, should be deemed as the best of all love-mixtures. By eating every day a quantity of Vidari, Ucchata and Masha, with sugar and thickened milk, a man would feel strong enough to visit a hundred women in a single night.

A woman, eager to be the mother of a child, should take every day, a quantity of thickened milk saturated with powdered Gulma, Masha, sesamum, and Vrihi grass, and the expressed juice of the roots of Vaishnavi, Shri, Bamboo, Darbha and Ashvattha. A similar result would be obtained by using the expressed juice of the roots of Durva and Ashvagandha, taken through the medium of thickened milk. A potion consisting of thickened milk and clarified butter, and treated with the essence of Kounti, Lakshmi, Shipha, Dhatri, Vajra, Lodhra, and the tender shoots of a Vata tree, should be used by a woman during her menses, whereby she would conceive and give birth to a male child. Similarly a quantity of thickened milk, treated with the expressed juice of Bael roots and of the tender shoots of a Vata tree, should be taken by a woman each day, until she would be in the family way. In the alternative, she should use as snuff, or take a quantity of the expressed juice of tile Devi and the tender shoots of a Vata tree, or a quantity of thickened milk boiled and prepared with the expressed juice of the lotus roots and the tender shoots of an Ashvattha. The same effect would be produced by a compound, consisting of ordinary cow's milk boiled and prepared with the fruits and branches of a cotton plant (Karpasha), or by the expressed juice of the flowers of an Apamarga plant administered through the vehicle of the milk of a she buffalo (13-19).

A woman, in the imminent danger of a miscarriage of the womb, should be treated with a potion consisting of the essence of Utpala, Puspaksha, Lodhra, sandal-wood, and Shariva, administered with ordinary sugar and the washings of rice. A paste composed of Laja, Jasthi, Sita, Draksha, Shiva, honey, and clarified butter, should be applied constantly on her tongue, simultaneously with the preceding remedy, until symptoms of decided improvement would set in. A plaster composed of pasted Arudhashak, Langali, Kakamachi and Shipha, or of any one of these drugs, and applied over the region of womb of a pregnant woman suffering from the labours of childbirth, would ensure a safe and speedy delivery. The expressed juice of a red or a white Java flower should be held as a very efficacious remedy for a case of leucorrhoea, either with a red or a white discharge. A composition consisting of the expressed juice of Keshara, Vrihatiroots, Gopi, Yasthi, Trinam, and Utpalam, taken with oil and goat's milk, should be deemed as a very good restorer of hair. The same medicine should be used in a case of decay or falling off of the hair, where it would act as an elixir, and give fresh vigour to their growth. Oil prepared with the essence of Dhatri, Bhringa, Jasthi, Anjana fruits and an adaka measure of thickened milk, would marvellously help the growth of the hairs and eye-lashes (20-26).

"Om obeisance to the three-eyed deity. Preserve and preserve, grant and grant peace to the herds of cattle in this village, subdue and subdue, sever and sever, disperse and disperse the epidemic diseases that break out among the horned cattle. Hrum Fut to the god, who wields a trident and a discus, and lives surrounded by the bovine species.

May the mighty bell-eared manifestation of Shiva (Ghastakarna), who is the leader of a mighty hosts; and who is a hero and as such successfully combats with, and destroys the epidemic diseases that does havoc among the horned cattle, preserve me." The above two cattle-preserving Mantras, as well as the two present couplets, should be made use of in the rite of Nyasa, practised for the welfare of the bovine species in general (27-28).

XXII

THE MANTRAS SACRED TO THE GOD SHIVA

SAID THE GOD OF FIRE:-

The Mantra, sacred to the god Shiva, consists of five letters in the original, and runs as, "Obeisance to Shiva," and which is sure to confer the god's own bliss on the votary. The man, who worships any of the manifestations of the god, such as Taraka, etc., is sure to be merged in the Supreme Brahma. The votary should contemplate the Supreme Brahma, who is the perfect knowledge, and the highest intelligence, as identical with the divine self of the mighty Shiva. Bramha and the other gods are but the different manifestations of Shiva. The five letters of the Shiva Mantra, have given birth to the five forms of the original cosmic matter. The senses proper, and the five proper sensibles have emanated from the essence of those five mystic letters. The five vital winds, the five senses of cognition, as well as the five senses of action, are but the reflection of those five letters. These letters, as well as the Mantra consisting of eight letters, should be deemed as the prototypes of the supreme Brahma (1-4).

The place of initiation should be washed with a composition of the five substances, that are prepared out of the milk of a cow, and consecrated with the god's own Mantra. Then having taken all the essential articles of worship to the place, the preceptor should practise the rites of Murtinyasa and Anganyasa, and scatter handsful of consecrated rice all over the spot. Subsequent to that, he should cook the sacrificial porridge, and divide it into three equal parts.

The first part should be dedicated to the god, with the second he should perform the Homa ceremony, while the third should be reserved for him and his disciple. Then having rinsed his mouth with water in the orthodox fashion, and evoked the different phases of beatitude in the body of his disciple, the preceptor should make over to him, a twig of the Kshira tree, to brush his teeth with. Then having cleansed his teeth and washed his mouth, he should throw down the twigs on the floor of the sacrificial shed. Then the preceptor should tie up the tuft of hair on the crown of his disciple, and exert a psychic preservative influence on him. Then the disciple, should lie down on the kusha mattress, spread on the sacrificial platform, with the preceptor. Then at dawn, the preceptor should inform him of the omens he had dreamt in the previous night. Then the Mandala laid out in the form known as the Sarvatobhadra-Mandalam, should be worshipped, for the realisation of all objects (5-11).

Then having practised the rite of ablution with clay, and consecrated the body with the Shiva-Mantra, the disciple should convert his hand into what is technically known as the Shivatirtha, and bathe by repeating the Aghamarshana (sin-absolving) Mantras. After that, he should commence the rite of worship, and sit in the posture known as the Padmasanam, by repeating the principal (Vija) Mantra. The rites of Puraka and Kumbhaka, should be practised with repetitions of the same Mantra, and he should merge his whole personality in the soul-light that pervades the upper region of his brain, to the extent of twelve fingers. Then having purified his own physical body, already burnt down with the essence of the Agni-

Mantra, he should bathe his innerself with the flow of ambrosia that would result from a practice of the abovesaid Pranayama.

Then having evoked his true divine self within his body, the preceptor should practise the rite of Anganyasa with the component letters of the Vija-Mantra, which are possessed of black, white, golden, red, and yellow colours respectively. Then having performed the rites of Murtinyasa and Pithanyasa as before, he should practise the rite of Nyasa in honour of the goddesses of energy presiding over the different petals of the psychic lotus-cushion spread in his heart for receiving the imaged divinity as follows:- "Om, obeisance to the goddess Vama, seated on the eastern petal of the lotus of the heart. Om, obeisance to the goddess Jestha seated on the southern petal. Om, obeisance to the goddess Kali seated on the south western petal. Om, obeisance to the goddess Kalavikarini seated on the western petal. Om, obeisance to the goddess Valavikarini seated on the north-western petal. Om, obeisance to Valapramathini seated on the northern petal. Om, obeisance to Sarva Bhutadamani seated on the north-eastern petal, and Om, obeisance to the goddess Manonmayee seated at its centre." Then the goddesses of light such as Shveta, Rakta, Sita, Pita, Shyama, Vanhinibha, Krishna and Aruna, should be worshipped in succession (12-22).

Then having brought the image of the evoked divinity out of the psychic lotus in the heart, the exterior lines of which are formed of the essence of the sun and the moon, etc., the preceptor, should contemplate it as placed on the external mystic diagram, laid out on the ground. Then he should practise the rite of Murtinyasa on the petals of the lotus as follows:—"Om, obeisance to Tatpurusha, who is of a white complexion. Om, obeisance to Aghora, who is possessed of eight hands and a black complexion. Om, obeisance to the four-faced and four-handed deity, and Om, obeisance to Sadyo jata at the west, etc." Then the different manifestations of the god, such as Vamadeva, Strivilashi, Panchasya, Ishana, Ananta, and Sukshma, etc., should be worshipped in succession. Similarly the gods such as Siddheshvara, Ekanetra, etc., should be worshipped in the east, while the gods such as Ekarudra, Trinetra, Shrikantha, and Shikhandi$_3$ as well as the regents of the cushion, such as Shveta, Pita, Sita, Rakta, Dhumra, etc., should be worshipped at its angular points (27-28).

Then the four hands of the god, together with the trident, the thunderbolt, the bow, and his four faces, and the manifestations, such as Umesha, Chandesha, Nandi, Isha, Mahakala, Ganeshvara, the bull, Bhringi, Skanda, etc., should be also worshipped. Then the thunderbolt, the spear, the club, the sword, the noose, the banner, the trident, and the discus, should be worshipped, after having worshipped the god in the east (29-31).

Then the disciple, duly fasting and consecrated, should be told to take nothing but Panchagvya that day. Then having rinsed his face, the preceptor should look steadfast at the eyes of his disciple, and cause it to be tied up (fastened) with the essence of the Netra-Mantra. Then having entered the disciple through the gate of the sacrificial shed, he should cause him to occupy a Darbha-seat on his right hand side, previously purified. Then having evoked the different principles of ether, etc., and the entire phases of beatitude in the innerself of the disciple, he should cause them to be merged in the principle of the Supreme Bramha, subsequently evoked therein by an act of Nyasa. Then he should cause the disciple to circumbulate the sacrificial shed. Then having entered him again through the western door of the Mandala, he should cause him to throw handsful of flowers on the ground. The spiritual name of the disciple should commence with the first letter of the name of the thing, the first flower would fall upon (32-36).

Then having lighted the fire in the sacrificial fire-pit provided with a rim and an aperture for outflow, and excavated beside the sacrificial ground, the preceptor should consecrate it with the Shiva-Mantras, and worship it conjointly with his disciple. Then having again evoked the above said principles in the order of their previous merging, he should cause them to permeate the blended palms of his disciple, on which he should spread the blades of consecrated Kusha-grass. Then he should cause libations of clarified butter to be poured on the sacred fire, a hundred times in honour of the principles of Earth, etc., by repeating the Hrid-Mantras. Then having again performed the Homa with a repetition of the ether-Vija, he should close the ceremony with the final libations consecrated with the Astra-Mantra, and which are known as the Homas of expiation. Then having worshipped the water-pitcher stowed at the centre of the sacrificial shed, he should cause the disciple to be bathed with its contents, and dictate the rules of conduct to be observed by the latter. Then the preceptor should worship his own Guru with offerings of gold, etc. Thus the rite of spiritual initiation, known as the Panchakshari Diksha, should be performed. The procedure laid down above, would hold good in cases of initiation, where the tutelary gods would be Vishnu, etc., (37-41).

XXIII

THE RECITATION OF THE FIFTY NAMES OF VISHNU

SAID THE GOD OF FIRE:–

A man, by reciting the following fifty names of Vishnu, would attain greater merit than by repeating the Mantras held sacred to that divinity. These names recited at holy pools and sanctuaries, prove eight times more meritorious. The Pundarikaksha (lotus-eyed) manifestation of the god, should be contemplated at the holy shrine of Pushkara, the Gadadhara (club-wielding) manifestation at Gaya, the Raghava manifestation on the summit of the mount Chitrakuta, the Daityasudana (demon-destroyer) manifestation at Prabhasa, the Jaya (the victor) manifestation at Jayanti, the Jayanta manifestation at the holy city of Hastinapura, the Varaha (boar) manifestation at Bardhamana, the Chakrapani (the discus-wielding) manifestation in Cashmere, the Janardana (the slayer of Jana) manifestation at Kuvjabhra, the Keshava (who lies on the water of first cause) manifestation at Mathura, the Hrishikesha manifestation at Kuvjabhraka the Jatadhara (the one with the clotted hairs) manifestation at the spot where the Ganges empties herself into the sea;

the Mahayoga manifestation in the village of Shalagrama, the god Hari on the holy mount of Govardhana, the Chaturvahu (four-armed) manifestation at Pindaraka, and Shankhi (wielder of a conch-shell) manifestation at Shankhadvara (1-5).

Similarly, a man should recite the name of the dwarf manifestation while staying within the holy precincts of Kurukshetra, contemplate the Trivikrama manifestation on the banks of the Yamuna, the Vishveshvara manifestation on the banks of the Shona, and the Kapila incarnation of the god at the shores of the Eastern sea. Likewise, a man should recite the name of Vishnu at the shore of the great ocean, as well as at the estuary of the Ganges. The Vanamala (the god with the garland of wild flowers) manifestation of the god, should be meditated upon in the country of Kishkindhya, the Deva at Raivataka; the Mahayoga manifestation at Benares, and the Ripunjaya (the victor of enemies) manifestation at Viroja, the Ajita (invincible) manifestation at Vishakayupa, and the Lokabhavana manifestation at Nepal. In the same way, a man should contemplate the god Krishna at Dvaraka, the god Madhusudana at Mandara, the god Ripuhara (killer of enemies) at Lokakula, and the god Hari at Shalagram. The Purusha is the deity which should be meditated upon at the holy shrine of Purusha Vata. One should contemplate the god Jagatprabhu (lord of the universe) at Vimala, the god Ananta (Infinite) in the forest of Saindhava, the god Sharngadhari (the wielder of a bow) in the forest of Dandaka, the god Shouri at the shore of the whirlpool known as the Utpalavartaka, the god Shriya-pati (the husband of the goddess Lakshmi) at the banks of the Nermada, the god Damodara on the summit of the holy Raivataka, the god Jalashayin at Nandaka, the god Gopishvara (the lord of the milk maids) at the shore of the Sindhvabdhi, the god Achyuta on the top of the holy hill Mahendra, the god of the gods on the peak of the mount Sajhya, and the god Vaikuntha in the forest of Madhava (several editions read Magadha (6-12).

The all-sin expiating epithet of the god should be recited on the summits of the Vindhaya mountains, the Purushottama epithet in the country of Orissa, while the universal soul should be deemed as running through the hearts of all. The man who recites, in an earnest spirit, the epithets enumerated above, would be able to enjoy all comforts in this life and to attain salvation in the next. Wherever there is a Vatatree, the Fire-god should be deemed as lying inherent therein. The god Shiva should be deemed as present in all walled quadrangles, the Rama manifestation of Vishnu as presiding over all hill-tops, while the god Madhusudana (the slayer of the demon Madhu) as pervading the whole universe. A man by meditating on Nara manifestation on earth, and on the god Garudadhvaja in heaven,, and on the god Vasudeva at all places, is sure to he blest with all earthly possessions, and salvation after death. A man by repeating the abovesaid epithets of Vishnu, become entitled to all bliss. Acts of Shraddha, gifts, or of mental repetition of a Mantra, become a million times more meritorious, if practised and performed at the holy shrines and sanctuaries mentioned above. A man, by departing this life in any of the above said places, is sure to be merged in the essence of the Supreme Bramha. The man, who personnally repeats these epithets, or hears them repeated by others, becomes pure in spirit, and ascends heaven after death

(13-17).

XXIV

THE INCANTATION FOR STUPETYING THE FACULTIES OF ADVERSARIES

SAID THE GOD OF FIRE:—

Hear me discourse on the Mantras, which are to be made use of in incantations, which are practised either for stupefying the faculties of one's adversaries, or for the purpose of creating dissensions between a hitherto fondly attached couple, or with a view to bring out one's death, or in order to drive a man distracted and crazed from his own hearth and home, or for the object of bringing disease upon one's enemy, as well as on those that can set them at nought (1).

"Om obeisance to the god Rudra, dancing in a frantic rage. Stupefy and stupefy the senses of such and such a person. Make him quit his hearth and home, and roam about as an aimless vagrant. Threaten him and threaten him. Hurl and hurl him aloft with thy fierce energy. Hrum. Fut. Tha. Tha."

The above Mantra repeated by a man at midnight in a cremation ground, followed by three hundred thousand oblations of Dhurta twigs, soaked in clarified butter and poured on the blazing fire of a burning funeral pile, tends to drive a person crazy from his home, against whom such an incantation is practised. An image of the enemy, should be made of the clay known as the Hemagairika, which should be pricked along the throat, or the heart, with a needle, charmed with the abovesaid Mantra, whereby his death would be the result. A philter composed of the ashes of a cremation ground, powered Brahmadandi, Markati, and Kharavala, charmed with the above Mantra, and strewn over the head, or over the housetop of one's enemy, would send him distracted and mad (2-4).

The rite of Nyasa should be practised with the Vijas, known as the Bhrigu, the ether, the fire, the Bhrigu, the fire, and the Varuna Vijas, in the following way:- "Hrung, Fut to the Achakra revolving over the reigon of the Sahasrara, (*corpora quadrigamina*). Obeisance to the god Shiva who is the regent of the psychic ganglion situated at the heart. Obeisance to the Chakra revolving over the tuft of hair on my crown. Obeisance to the Sanchakra which serves me as a weapon." The rite of Nyasa should be practised as before in connection with the Jvala-Chakra. The weapons of the god Vishnu, such as the bow, known as the Sharanga, and the discus. Sudarshana, should be deemed as the neutralisers of all fell charms and incantations. The votary should imagine the component letters of the Chakra Vija, as severally located in his head, eyes, face, heart, arms, and the legs.

Then the rite of Murtinyasa, should he practised as follows:- "The god with a set of fierce and diabolical teeth, should be contemplated as seated on the nave of the fiery circle, and as wielding in his four arms, such flowers and weapons, as:the conchshell, the discus, the mace, the lotus, the spear, and the bow. The eyes and the hairs of the god should be contemplated as of a dark amber colour, and his cushion should be imagined, as radiating columns of fire and energy along its spokes, which are dealing destruction to all sorts of diseases and malignant planets. The discus, should be contemplated as made of a yellow light, the mace of a dark red, while the succeeding arms, should be alternately contemplated as of a sky blue tint (5-9).

The exterior periphery of the discus, should be contemplated as made of a consolidated dazzling white light, gradually modified in a brown, and ultimately merging in a dark black colour. The two inner peripheries should be contemplated as burning with a sky blue lustre. Then having brought a pitcherful of a water, and seen the mighty discus (Sudarshanam) reflected therein with the aid of the inner eye, the preceptor should offer libations to that celestial weapon at the south.

The libations should consist of clarified butter made out of cow's milk, and of sacrificial porridge containing the twigs of an Apamarga plant, sun-dried rice, sesamum, and mustard, and should be poured on the sacrificial fire to the number of thousand and eight. The preceptor should then again pour into the pitcher the remnants of the offerings in due order, and locate therein the energies of the gods, such as Vishnu, etc. by an act of psychic attraction.

"Obeisance to the deities who attend upon the god Vishnu, and who are the givers of all and universal peace. Accept these offerings. Obeisance to the goddess of peace." The final obiation should be consecrated with the abovesaid Mantra, and cast with the remnant of the abovesaid water of libation (10-14).

The Homa ceremony, should be performed at the

four cardinal points of the mystic diagram with jets of Panchagavya, poured on the fire with the branches of a Palasha or a Kshira tree, previously kept immersed in pitchers containing the same substance. The Brahmanas who would officiate at the ceremony, should be rewarded with satisfactory remunerations; and both these Homas should be deemed as very effective neutralisers of spells and incantations. The Homa should be performed with the bunches of Durva grass, where the ceremony would be undertaken for increasing the duration of one's life. The oblations of lotus flowers, should be cast in the sacrificial fire, for the increase of one's possessions, while the Homa should be performed with the twigs of an Oudumvara tree for the birth of a son. The libations should be poured on the fire in a cattle house, where the general increase and multiplication of the horned species would be desired, while in Homas performed for the expansion of one's intellect, the twigs of all sorts of trees, should be used for casting the libations (15-17).

"Om, Kshoum, obeisance to the god Narasinha, burning with his own scorching effulgence, and whose eyes pour forth torrents of living fire, matched only by the glen of his burning diabolical teeth. Obeisance to the destoryer of all demons, to the slayer of all ghosts, to the destroyer of all sorts of fever. Burn and burn, cook and cook, preserve and preserve. Hrung-Fut."

The above Mantra, sacred to the Narasinha, should be deemed as the remover of all distempers. The above Mantra, duly repeated, tends to set at naught all sorts of spells and charms and the evil influences of malignant planets, as well as the cases which give birth to epidemics or pestilential diseases. By rubbing over the body the marrow of a frog, consecrated with the above Mantra, one is sure to walk unscathed through fire (18).

XXV

THE MANTRAS BY WHICH THE THREE WORLDS CAN BE ENCHANTED

SAID THE GOD OF FIRE:—

Now I shall narrate to you the Mantra, or the means by which the three worlds can be enchanted, and due repetition of which leads to the attainment of the fourfold bliss (Chaturvarga).

"Om, Hreem, Shreem, Hreem, Hrum. Om, obeisance. O thou, who art the best of beings, the prototype of the grandest subjectivity, and in whom the goddess of beauty and plenty (Lakshmi) has her abode, O thou, who dost agitate the whole universe and openest the hearts of all maidens, and dost intoxicate the inmates of the three worlds with the wine of love, dost thou heaten and heaten, agitate and agitate, attract and attract, rend asunder and rend asunder the hearts of gods, mortals, and the fair maids of the universe. O kill and kill, stupefy and stupefy their senses, illumine their hearts with the light of love and screw up their desires to the highest pitch. O thou the most bountiful giver of all good fortunes, the granter of all boons, kill and kill such and such a person with thy mace, sword and discus, hit him with all thy arrows, whril and whril him round with thy dreadful nooze, strike and strike with thy spear. Come, O come, why dolt thou tarry? Dost thou bide the time, till I attain my success with this incantation? Hrung, Fut, Obeisance."

The rite of Nyasa in connexion with the Mantra, should be practised as follows:- "Om, O thou the best of men, the maddener of the three worlds. Hrung, Fut, Obeisance to thee, located in my heart. Dost thou attract and attract, O thou god of matchless prowess. Hrung, Fut and obeisance to thee who art to me as a weapon. O thou lord of the three worlds, strike and strike, cleave and cleave the mind of all, and bring them under my absolute control, Hrung, Fut, (obeisance) to thee who dost permeate my eyes. O thou charmer of the three worlds, O thou Hrishikesha, O thou, the matchles spirit, O thou who attractest the hearts of all women. Come and come, O god, I make obeisance to thee. The rites of Anganyasa, etc., should be practised like the one described in connexion with the principal Mantra enumerated above" (I).

Then having repeated it a five hundred times, and practised, a thousand times, the rite of Abhisheka in connexion therewith, the preceptor should prepare the sacrificial porridge on the fire kindled in the sacred firepit, and pour on it a hundred libations, consisting of clarified cow butter. Libations consisting of curd, clarified butter, thickened milk, sacrificial porridge and milk, should be separately poured on the sacred fire. Twelve libations should be cast into the fire, by repeating the principal Mantra, and a thousand such, after that, containing sesamum and sun-dried rice. Subsequent to that, oblations composed of barley, the three sweets, fruits and flowers, should be cast into the fire by way of competing the ceremony (2-4).

The votary should take himself the residue of the sacrificial porridge, poured on the fire in the course of the Homa. The preceptor and the Brahmanas should be feasted and made happy with remunerations, whereby the incantation would take effect. Then having bathed and rinsed his mouth in the orthodox fashion, the votary should observe a vow of silence, enter the chamber of sacrifice, sit with crossed legs in the posture known as the Padmasanam, and then practise the rite of Bhutashuddhi (purification of the material principles of the body). The celestial discus, Sudarshanam, should be contemplated as guarding the different quarters of the sky, and, as such, barring the intrusions of the interrupting ghosts and malignant spirits on the sacred precincts of the chamber of sacrifice. Then the rite of Nyasa should be practised as follows:—The votary should contemplate the Vija-Mantra Ram, which burns with a fierce dusky glare, as located in the region of his umbilicus, by which his body would be absolved of all sins and impieties. Similarly, the Vija-Mantra Ram, should be imagined as located in the lotus of the heart (solar pelxus), and as darting rays of fire in all directions, and consuming the impious principles of the body. The ambrosia shed down from the lotus of the brain, should be contemplated as dropping down by the way of the mystic nerve Sushumna, and permeating the whole body.

Thus having purified the body, the votary should practise the rite of Pranyam described before, by thrice repeating the Mula-Mantra. Then having brought down the psychic energy from the effulgent mystic ganglion of the brain, and located it in the different parts of his body as the arms, the neck, the heart, the sides, in short, all through his body, the votary should meditate upon the universal soul, by repeating the Pranava-Mantra, as follows:-

> "We know the charmer of the three worlds, let our mind meditate on his divine self, may Vishnu lead our minds to dwell on that"(5-11).

Then having finished the soul-worship, the votary should sprinkle water on the vessels of divine service, and the articles to be used in its course. After that, the soul should be drawn out by an act of psychic abstraction, and he should place and formally worship it on the sand-cushion, spread out on the ground. The Pitha or the cushion of the god, consisting of the contrary principles of virtue and vice, etc., should be imagined as grown over by a gigantic lotus flower, on which the god, manifest in the shape of a youth of beautiful form, and glowing with the gladsome light of youth and beauty, with large red-striped eyes rolling with the intoxication of love and desire, and smiling with the smiling flowers of the heaven that had been threaded into a garland that dangles over his celestial garments, dipped in the yellow haze of an autumn morning, should be imagined as seated and attended upon by his divine companions. The god should be imagined as effulgent like the combined lustre of a thousand suns, extremely beautiful, compassionate towards all, wielding the five specific darts of cupid in his two or four hands, and surrounded on all sides by a bevy of celestial beauties, with his eyes rivetted on the fair face of his beloved Lakshmi (12-16).

The specific weapons of the god, such as the discus, the conchshell, the bow, the sword, the spear, the Mushula, the club, and the noose, should be worshipped. The goddess Lakshmi, should be imagined as seated on the left thigh of the god, and entwining her hands round his neck, and holding a full-blown lotus-flower in her hand, and clinging close to the bosom of her beloved husband with her full developed breast, and bedecked with the diamond Kousthubha. The ring like curls, known as the Shrivatsa, should be worshipped conjointly with the god Hari, clad in yellow garments wearing a garland of wild flowers, and wielding in his hands a conchshell, a discus, etc.

"Oum, O thou Sudurshana, O thou king of all the quoits, O thou who art the dread to the evil-doers, cleave and cleave, cut and cut, rend asunder and rend asunder the mighty incantations practised by others. Devour and devour them. Eat and eat them up, curse and curse them. Hrung Fut, obeisance to Jalachara. O thou, keen-edged sword, cut and cut. I make obeisance to the great sword. Hung-Fut (obeisance) to the bow Sharanga, stretched with its arrow, Hung-Fut."

"We contemplate the nature of the concourse of physical forces. We meditate on the principle of the fourfold attributes. May the supreme Bramha lead our mind to dwell on the same."

"O Samvartaka, come neighing in thunder, reverse the order of Nature, make her stand aghast, and recoil on her visible material self, Hrung-Fut. I make obeisance to thee, O thou Mace, bind and bind, attract and attract. I have subdued thee with the potency of the Hrung-Vija, cut and cleave with the spear, as thou art under my control by the agency of the same Mantra. The weapons imagined as wielded by the god in his four arms, should be worshipped with the abovesaid Mantras, respectively held sacred to them" (17-19).

"Am, obeisance to the king of birds (Hrum-Fut.)"

The celestial bird, Tarksha who carries the god on his shoulders, as well as the Anga Devatas, should be worshipped with the abovesaid Mantra in the different petals of the mystic lotus. The goddesses of energy, such as Pita. Lakshmi, Sarasvati, Rati, Priti, Jaya, Sita, Kirti, Kanti, Shyama, Tusti, Pusti, Smarodita, as well as the Lokapalas (the regents of the different worlds), should be worshipped in the mystic diagram, specifically held sacred to the god, in which the Tarkshas should be imagined as blowing chowries unto that divinity. A worship of Vishnu, made as above indicated, should be performed for the perfect fruition of the charm. The Mantra, running as "Om Shrim, Krim, Hreem, Hum obeisance to Vishnu, who is the charmer of the three worlds," should be mentally repeated after the worship; and the rites of subsequent Homa and Abhisheka, should be performed with the same Mantra. A man, by worshipping the god, as above indicated, becomes entitled to all sorts of bliss. The goddess of charm should be propitiated, every day, with libations of water and offerings of flower, till the spell would take effect, and by repeating the abovesaid Mantra. The abovesaid Vija-Mantra, should be repeated three hundred thousand times, and a hundred thousand libations of clarified butter containing the twigs of a Vilva tree, should be pouted on the tire by repeating the same. Libations containing rice, fruits, perfumes, or the blades of Durva grass poured on the fire, as in the one described in the preceding line, would increase the duration of the life of the votary, as similar rites of Homas and Abhishekas are always crowned with the fulfilment of one's desires.

"Om obeisance to the boar manifestation of Vishnu, the lord of the regions of Bhu, Bhuba Sva, etc. Grant me the universal sovereignty as my heart desires. I make obeisance to thee." A man, by repeating ten thousand times, every day, the abovesaid Mantra, is sure to be crowned as the king of his country (20-26).

XXVI

THE MANTRAM SACRED TO THE GODDESS OF FORTUNE

SAID THE GOD OF FIRE:–

The Vija-Mantra, Shreem, is sacred to the goddess of fortune, and grants to its repeat all success in life. The Mantra runs as "I make Obeisance to the great goddess of beauty, the goddess of complete victory and success, and to the deity who is effulgent as the flash of lightning." The rite of Anganyas, which consists of nine Mantras in the present case, should be practised in its entirety while any of the said Mantras should be repeated." The Mantra runs as:—"Obeisance to the goddess Shree, who is the goddess of victory. Bind and bind down (my enemies), O thou possessed of mighty prowess. I make obeisance to thee, Hrung. O thou possessed of an enormous body and who dost wield a lotus flower in thy hand, Hrung-Fut, I make obeisance to thee. O thou, goddess of beauty and wealth, Fut (obeisance) to the goddess Shree. Obeisance to Shree, and Fut to the principle of splendour which she represents. Obeisance to Shree and to the grantor of beauty, Svaha, Shree, Fut" (1).

The above Mantra should be counted a hundred thousand, or three hundred thousand times on a rosary of Aksha or lotus-seeds, whereby the repeater would grow richer every day. The goddess Shree should be worshipped with the abovesaid Mantra, either in a temple dedicated to Vishnu, or in one consecrated with the presence of her own image, by which the possessions of the worshipper would grow more and more every day. A person, wishing to subjugate the mind of the sovereign of his country, or an all-round improvement of his social status, should pour on the sacrificial fire kindled with the twigs of a Catechu tree, a hundred thousand libations of clarified butter containing grains of sun-dried rice. The rite of Abhisheka performed with the washings of Mustard seeds, and a repetition of the above-said Mantra, would neutralise the baneful influences of all malignant planets and harmful incantations. A hundred thousand twigs of a Vilva tree soaked in clarified butter, and poured on the sacred fire by repeating the same Mantra, would give a better turn to one's fortune (2-5).

Then the votary should imagine that an open hall of rectangular structure, had been erected in the region of his heart, with a door or an opening on each of its four sides. The goddesses of energy, such as Valaka, Vamana, and Shyama, etc., should be imagined as guarding the eastern entrance of the hall, and dancing with uplifted hands, carrying in them the festoons of white lotus flowers. The goddess Vanamalini should be imagined as possessed of a snow-white complexion and as carrying red lotus flowers in her hands, and dancing in same posture at the door at the south. The goddess Vibhishika, should be contemplated as possessed of a green complexion and carrying white lotus flowers in her hands, and dancing in the same posture at the door at the west. Lastly the goddess Shankari, should be contemplated as guarding the door at the north, in the manner similar to what has been described in the case of her sister goddesses. A mystic lotus of eight petals, should be imagined as to have sprung from the centre of that hall, and the different manifestations of Vishnu, such as Vasudeva, Sankarshana, Pradyumna, and Aniruddha, should be contemplated as wielding the conch shell, the discus, the mace and the lotus - flowers in their hands, and as seated on the four petals of the lotus respectively pointing towards the four cardinal points of the sky. The celestial elephants, who guard the eight apertures of the heaven, such as Anjana, Kashmira, Surasa, Kshira, and Kuruntaka etc., should be contemplated as carrying golden pitchers with their trunks, and blocking the regions of heaven with their massive silver frames (6-11)

The goddess Shree, should be contemplated as seated on the bed of polens of the lotus, and as possessed of a golden complexion and four arms, the two right and the two left, being imagined as bent in the attitude of encouragement and benediction. The goddess, should be further contemplated, as clad in a while garment of an extremely, white texture and scented with lotus flowers.

The man, who worships the goddess and her companion divinities, becomes possessed of all good things in this life. The votary should never put on his head, such flowers, etc., as the lotus, the Drona, and the leaves of a Vilva tree. Further he should recite the vedic verses known as the Shri-shuktas from the eighth or the twelfth day of a lunar month, taking nothing but the sacred Payasha during the entire period of recitation. The god, should be worshipped with the rites of invocation and farewell, and libations consisting of the twigs of a Vilva tree and lotus flowers, and Payasha, should be separately poured on the fire in honour of the goddess (12-16).

The Mantra known as the Durga-Hridaya, runs as follows:—"Om, Hreem, to thee, O goddess, who hast slain the great buffalo-demon in a single combat, Tha, Tha, to thee, who art his sworn enemy. O thou, the enemy of the buffalo-demon, disperse and disperse. (Hung-Fut Tha, Tha,) the buffalo-demon, over-power and overwhelm him with ruin. Hung, kill and kill the buffalo, Hung, O thou goddess who hast slain the buffalo, Fut." The goddess should be worshipped by repeating the abovesaid Mantras, as well as those which are known as the Sangas, after having performed the rite of cushion worship. Om Hreem, obeisance to thee, O Durga, who art the protectress of the three worlds. Obeisance to Durga. Then the rites of worship should be performed on the different petals of the mystic diagram as follows:—Obeisance to Varavarni, obeisance to Arya. Obeisance to

Kanakaprabha, obeisance to Krittika, obeisance to Abhayaprada. "Obeisance to Kanyaka, and obeisance to Krittika. Obeisance to the goddess who removes all causes of fear, obeisance to Kanyaka, and obeisance to Sarupa." These divinities should be worshipped on the petals of the mystic lotus, and by repeating the Vijas, which are respectively held sacred to them. The weapons of the goddess, should be Worshipped, as obeisance to the discus, obeisance to the conch-shell, obeisance to the mace, obeisance to the sword, obeisance to the bow, and obeisance to the arrow. The goddess Durga, who is the greatest of all peace-making divinities, should be worshipped on the eighth day of the increase of the moon's phase. A worship of the goddess Durga, leads to victory, and increases the duration of the life of the worshipper and makes him a favourite with his master (17-19).

A rite of Homa performed with the Susaddhya-Mantra sacred to the god Ishana, and with libations of clarified butter containing sesamum, should be deemed as the best of charms. Similarly, the rites of Homa performed in connection with the abovesaid worship, and with oblations of lotus-flowers poured on the fire, are sure to lead the performer to victory and fame, while those performed with the oblations of Palasha twigs, or the bunches of Durva grass, should be deemed as the peace-givers, and the fulfillers of all desires. The Homa in connection with the above worship, and in course of which oblations of crow's wings are poured on the fire, is sure to bring death and confusion to the person against whom it should be practised. A repetion of the Mantra, running as,-" Om obeisance (Svaha) to the goddess

Durga, to the goddess Durga who is the protectress of all creatures," should be,deemed as a safeguard against all sorts of incantations and the evil effects of malignant planets. The goddess, should be contemplated as possessed of a bluish complexion and four arms, respectively wielding in them a conch-shell, a discus, a lotus, a spear, a sword, and a trident, and looking fierce and dreadful in a fit of bursting rage. The above manifestation of the goddess, should be worshipped before commencing a battle, together with her swords and other engines of warfare, by which the votary is sure to be crowned with victory (2~23).

"Om Obeisance to the goddess Jvala-Malini (glowing with the tongues of living fire) who is surrounded by a pack of jackals and vultures, etc., Obeisance and obeisance (Tha, Tha) to the protectress." The above Mantra, should be repeated before marching out in a battle, by which the votary would return victorious and laden with glory (24).

XXVII

THE MANTRA FOR WORSHIPPING THE GODDESS TVARITA WHO GRANTS ENJOYMENT OF EARTHLY COMFORTS AND SALVATION OFTER DEATH

SAID THE GOD OF FIRE:—

Now I shall describe the mode of worshipping the goddess Tvarita, who grants to her votary, the enjoyment of earthly comforts and salvation after death.

"Om obeisance to the divine energy which pervades all receptacles (Adhara-Shakti). Om Hrum, Pum, Pum, obeisance to the great lion. Om, obeisance to the lotus flowers. Om, Hreem, Hrum, Khecha, Cheksha, Hrum, Kshaim Hrum Fut, obeisance to the goddess Tvarita, Khecha, obeisance to the heart. Chechha, obeisance to the head, Cheksha, obeisance to the tuft of hair on the crown, Kshapustri, obeisance to the energy of the Mantra that protects me as an armour. Hrum, Hrum, obeisance to the eyes. Hrum, Kshaim obeisance to the Astra (weapon).

The Gayatri Mantra which is specifically sacred to the goddess runs as follows:-

"Om, we know the Tvarita Vidya, let us meditate on the Turna Vidya. May the goddess lead our mind to dwell on the same." Obeisance to Shripranita, obeisance to Hrungkara, Om, Khi Cha, obeisance to the heart. Obeisance to the goddess Khechari. Om, obeisance to Chanda, obeisance to Chhedini, obeisance to Kshepani, obeisance to Stri and Hrungkari, obeisance to the goddess of compassion, obeisance to the goddess of success, obeisance to the goddess of victory, obeisance to Kinkara. Protect and protect me. Om stay here and be steadist as commanded by the goddess Tvarita. Obeisance. The goddesses who preside over the present form of incantation, are known as Totala, Tvarita, Turna, etc., (1).

Then the votary should contemplate the component letters of the Mantra, as located in the regions of his head, eyebrows, neck, heart, navel, arms, thighs, knee-joints, and legs by an act of Nyasa.

The goddess should be contemplated as possessed of a golden complexion, and dressed as a huntress of the mountainous regions. She should be contemplated as clad in a garment of leaves tied round her waist, with a crown of peacok's feathers set on her graceful head. She should be further contemplated as seated on a throne, shaded over by an umbrella of peacock's plumes, and wearing a garland of wild flowers. The bracelets and anklets of the goddess, should be imagined as made of snakes. Having thus contemplated the presence of the goddess, the votary should repeat, a million times, the Mantra held sacred to her. The god Isha became a hunter in ancient time, and so his goddess used to dress herself in the guise of a huntress. The man who worships, or meditates upon the divine huntress, or repeats the Mantra specifically held sacred to her, is sure to be successful in all his undertakings. Such a worship is calculated as an active counteracting agent in all cases of poisoning or snakebite, etc., (2-7).

A lotus shaped diagram, containing eight petals, should be inscribed in a square delineated on the ground, each side, of which would contain a door or an aperture. The Vija, Hrung, should be written on each of the eight petals, while the Vija, Hring, should be written on the centre. Then the rite of Sadanga worship, should be performed on the petals, commencing from the one at the east, and by repeating the Mantras, such as obeisance to the Gayatri and the heart, and so on. The goddess Fatkari, wielding a bow and an arrow in her hands, should be worshipped outside the gate of the Yantra, the goddesses Jaya and Vijaya, should be worshipped at the gates, while the Kinkaras, each wielding a club, etc., should be worshipped outside the border line of the mystic diagram.

Libations should be poured on the fire kindled in a fire-pit, shaped like the female organ of generation. Oblations of Arjuna twigs, should be cast into the fire, where the rite would be undertaken for the gain of gold, while the rite of Homa should be performed with oblations of wheat, or rice, where a general bettering of one's health and complexion, would be desired. Oblations composed of barley, rice and sesamum, and poured on the fire, as above indicated, should be deemed as the grantors of all success. Oblations consisting of Aksha seeds, or libations of blue vitrol, would bring about the destruction of one's enemy. Similarly the twigs of a Shalmali tree, used as oblations in a Homa of the above sort, would cut the thread of life of one's adversary. Oblations of Jamvu fruits would be crowned by the attainment of wealth and rice, while oblations of blue lotus flowers would establish a perpetual peace in one's household. Oblations of red lotus flowers, would be rewarded with a general ameliora, lion of one's health and fortune. Oblations of Kunda flowers would be rewarded with the elevation of one's status in life (8-13).

Similarly, oblations of Jessamine flowers should be deemed as powerful agents in creating unrest and discord in a household, while oblations of Kumuda flowers, would win for one the affections of his community. Oblations of Ashoka flowers would be rewarded with the birth of a son, while oblations of Patala flowers would win for the votary the hands of a fair maiden. Oblations of mango fruits, would increase the duration of the life of the votary. Oblations of sesamum seeds, would give a better turn to one's fortune, while oblations of Bael and Champaka, would be followed by a blessing of increased wealth and beauty. Oblations of Madhuka flowers, would be rewarded with the realisation of one's desires, while by oblations of Bael fruits the votary would become an omniscient being. By repeating three hundred thousand times the abovesaid Mantra, or by pouring three hundred thousand libations on the fire with same Mantra, or by simply meditating on its symbolised principle, a man may attain to all his objects. The worship, should be conducted on the Mandala, and twenty-five libations should be poured on the fire, by repeating the Gayatri, by way of completing the ceremony. Three hundred libations of clarified butter, should be poured on the fire, by repeating the principal Mantra. The rite of initiation should be conducted with the Pallava Mantras. The votary should take Panchagavya before the worship, and live on the sacrificial porridge during the day of ceremony (14-17).

XXVIII

THE WORSHIP OF THE GODDESS TVARITA BY WHICH ONE CAN ENJOY ALL COMFORTS IN THIS LIFE

SAID THE GOD OF FIRE:−

Now I shall narrate to you the process of worshipping the goddess Tvarita, by which a man is enabled to enjoy all the comforts which this life may possibly offer to an individual, and to attain to salvation after death. The image of the goddess, should be delineated with the specific dusts on the ground, inside a mystic diagram of the Vajra class. The diagram, should be embellished with corridors, and gates. The goddess, should be contemplated as possessed of eighteen hands, with her left knee-joint bent double and placed on the back of a lion, while the right one should be imagined as placed on the divine cushion. The goddess, should be further contemplated as embellished with the ornaments of snake. The nine right hands of the goddess, should be imagined as respectively armed with a thunderbolt, with a hollow vessel (Kunda), with a sword, with a discus, with a club, with a trident, with an arrow, and with a spear, the last being imagined as bent in the attitude of benediction. The nine left hands of the goddess, should be contemplated as armed with a bow, with a noose, with an arrow, with a bell, with a conchshell, with a spear, and with a thunder-bolt, respectively; the index finger of the fifth hand being imagined as held straight and pointed; and the eighth hand being contemplated as bent in the attitude of benediction (1-5)

Having worshipped the goddess, manifest in the shape as described above, a man should be able to kill his enemies and to win a kingdom at ease. Such a worship, in variably grants longevity to the worshipper, who becomes possessed of supernatural powers, and performs miracles in testimony of his superhuman attainments. Such a man is invincible in the seven nether regions, such as the Tala, etc., and reigns supreme and is almighty in the world like the fire, that would consume the universe on the day of the millenium (6-7).

Now I shall describe the mode of stringing together the Mantras that are held sacred to the goddess, and which consists in a process of elimination and coupling. First the vowel letters of the alphabet should be written on the ground, and then the palatal consonants such as the Ka Vargas. The third letter in the order of arrangement should be those which belong to the group known as the labio palatal. The fourth letter should be a dento-palatal one while the fifth should be a Dento-labial. The sixth Vija in the order of enumeration, should consist of eight letters. The letters of the seventh should belong to the group of Misra Varnas, arranged in the way technically known as the Sampata, while those of the eighth Vija should belong to the class, known as the Ushma Varnas. The entire Vija Mantra should be then constructed. The first Vija should begin with the sixth vowel letter of the Sanskrit alphabet, and end with the one of the Ushma class, coupled with the phonetic symbol of the nasal Chandravindu. The second set of the letters (Vijas), should belong to the group of palatals, coupled with the eleven vowel letters of the alphabet. The first letters of the second set should consist of letters solely belonging to the labio-palatal sounds, while those of its latter half, should be selected from the same group. After that, the letters of the palatal group, should be arranged commencing from its very beginning and respectively and successively coupled with the eleven vowel letters. After that should be written the second letter of the Ushma group successively coupled with the eleven vowel letters of the alphabet as before, and counted from the latter end of the list. The first letters of the next set of Vijas, should consist of two labio-dental sounds, counted from the latter end of the group, its latter part being composed of letters of the Mishra group, counted from its opposite end. The letters of the second group, should consist of the letters of the palatal group coupled with the fourth vowel letter of the alphabet, the latter part of the set being composed of the second letter of the Ushman class coupled with the eleven vowel letters in succession. The Mantra, thus composed and so strewn together, should be repeated by appending it to the Pranava Mantra, and by affixing the term Syaha (obeisance) to it, in all acts of pouring libations on the sacrificial fire (8-18).

The rite of Nyasa, in connection with the Mantra, should be performed as follows:- Om, Hreem, Hrum, Hrum, Hah (obeisance) to the region of the heart, permeated with the essence of these Mantras. Hrum, Hah (obeisance) to the region of the heart, permeated with the energy of the preceding Vijas. May the tuft of hair on my crown be permeated with the essence of the Mantra, running as Hrum, burn and burn. May the energy of the two Kulva Vijas protect my body as a coat of mail. May the energy of the Vija Mantra, Hreem, Shreem, Ksham, permeate the region of my eyes, both physical and spiritual. Kshoum, Hum, Khoum, Hum, fut (obeisance) to the spiritual weapon composed of the essense of these Mantras. The rite of Guhya Nyasa in connection with the Mantra, should be performed before the preceding one.

I shall presently narrate to you, the Mantras that are to be used in connection with the worship of the goddess Tvarita, as well as those that are known as the Vidyangas. The two Hrid-Mantras should be imagined as located in the region of the heart, twelve as filling in the region of the head, the Tara-Mantras as

Sacred words of Power

premeating the region of the eyes, the fifth and the sixth Vijas of the entire Mantra as premeating the tuft of the hair on the crown, and the seventh and eighth as protecting the body as a coat of mail. The name of the goddess which is to be mentioned first in connection with the above Mantra, is Totala, the next divinity, in relation to whom, the next rite should be practised, being the goddess with thunderbolt in her lips (Vajratunda) The latter rite should be performed with the Mantra consisting of the Vijas, and which runs as:—Kha, Kha, Hum, obeisance to the goddess Vajratunda. Then the rites of the subsequent Nyasa, should be performed as, Kha, Kha, Hum, obeisance to the goddess Indradutika (maiden messenger to the god Indra). Kha, Kha, Hum, obeisance to Khechari, Kha, Kha, Hum, obeisance to Jvalini, Varcha with (obeisance) to the Shara Vibhishini (the one threatening with a fierce arrow). Kha, Kha, (obeisance) to the goddess Shavari, (the divine huntress).' Chhe (obeisance) to Chhedini.' Chhe to Karalini (the dreadful one), Che Kha and Kha to Karali, Shreem to the goddess Shrava-Drava-Plavani, Kha Kha to the goddess Duti-Plava. Strim to the goddess who has created the eternal time. The same Vijas should be contemplated as located in the specific parts of the body as the prototypes of the goddesses known as Dhunani and Vasanavegika. Laugh and laugh, O thou goddess Kapila, who art also known by the epithets of Kshepaksha and Dutika. Hung "to the goddess of energy and light. Hung to the goddess who is the wife of Rudra. Hung to the goddess Matangi and to the goddess who is the maide messenger of the goddess Roudri. Kha Kha to the sword wielded by the mighty Tvarita, and Fut to the goddess who serves as the maiden envoy to the Supreme Brahma (19-27).

The votary should first imagine his body as fully permeated with the essence of the Hrid-Mantra, and subsequently with that of the one known as the Netra, from the head to the foot, and from the foot to the head. He should contemplate the members of his body, such as the legs, the knee-joints, the arms, the navel, the heart, the throat, the face, and the upper regions of the brain, as permeated with the energy of the principal Vija-Mantra, both along the ingoing and out-going currents of vitality. Then he should perceive the psychic hale, mellow and effulgent as the rising moon, as coming downwards from the lotus of the brain, and shedding ambrosia and carrying eternal life all through his body. The votary should locate the effulgent images of the principal Vija-Mantras in the different parts of his body, such as the head, the face, the throat, the heart, the navel and especially at the tips of his two index-fingers, by an act of psychic abstraction. The man, who perceives the moon in his head and the pyschic lotus situated at the lower part of his trunk, and knows his body as permeated with the essence of the congery of the abovesaid Mantras, knows no death or disease. Even the man, who meditates upon the divine self of the goddess as above indicated or repeats her name, at least, a hundred and eight times, after having purelised a rite of Nyasa in the way above enumerated, is rewarded with a similar fate (28-33).

Now I shall describe the different postures of the hand with which the presence of the goddess (Tvratia), is to be invoked before the commencement of the actual worship and which are known as the Pranitas, etc. The latter-named Mudra admits of a five-fold division. The first sort consists in firstly out-stretching the palms of the two hands, and in then putting them on the head, with the two index-fingers attached thereto, after having bent in two, the two thumbs and the two middle fingers. Two such folded palms carried down from the head, and placed on the region of the heart, with the little and middle fingers turned upward, and the index-finger placed beneath the latter, are known as the Savijas. The one in which the tip of the thumb is placed beneath, or at the root of the middle finger, is known as the Vedini (piercer) Mudra. The palm, folded in the same way, with the only distinction of the two up-lifted little fingers, is known as the Karali, the greatest of all the Mudras, and which should be carried up to the region of the heart, at the time of repeating any particular Mantra. The same Mudra, with the distinction of the two up-turned thumbs, is known as the Vajra, and should be placed on the part of the body, having the same designation. The Mudras, known as the Danda (club), the sword, the discus, and the mace, should be made to resemble in shape, the abovesaid weapons in reality. The Mudra known as the Trident, is formed by placing the thumb at the roots of the first three fingers, held in an upright position, while the one known as the spear, should be made by lifting up the two middle fingers only. The palm is usually enfolded in twenty-eight different postures or Mudras, such as the arrow, the hand of benediction or encouragement, the bow, the noose, the bell, the weight, the conch-shell, the mace, and the eight sorts of lotus. The five Mudra, known as the Mohini, the Mokshini, the Jvalini, the Amritamaya, and the Pranita, should be made use of, in the course of a rite of Homa, or worship (34-43).

XXIX

THE INCANTATIONS BY WHICH ONE CAN ACQUIRE LEARNING

SAID THE GOD OF FIRE:—

Now I shall enumerate the Vidya Prastara Mantras, and the rites of incantations which should be practised with them for the attainment of objects mentioned under each of them. The man, who knows these Mantras severally and in entirety, as well their arrangements in the different mystic triangular diagrams, or is conversant with their mode of repetition both in due and inverse orders, is sure to achieve the highest success in (connection with) his penances (1-3).

Many are the books of scriptures, and innurnerable are the congeries of Mantras which are to be found in them, and therefore it is most difficult to master their modes of application, or to find out the occasions on which they are to, he applied. The first letter of the Mantra, has a long sound, which should be dealt with later on. First I shall describe the mystic diagram, in the chambers of which the component letters of the Mantra, are to be arranged. Four parallel straight lines are to be drawn across four perpendicular parallels, so as to give rise to a quadrilateral figure, divided into nine chambers. Then a circle is to be described around the middle chamber, and the different letters of the Mantra, should be written in each of them. The man, who knows all about this mystic diagram, and of the Mantras written in its different chambers, should deem all sorts of supernatural powers as lying at his fingers ends. Such as a man is sure to receive the homage of the three regions, and to exercise sovereign powers over the nine continents of the world (4-8).

Having written the Siva Mantras all over the forehead of a human skull, the votary, should walk out and collect a piece of a deadman's cloth from a cremation ground. On it he should describe the mystic diagram sacred to the goddess as before described, and write the name of his antagonist in each of the petals of the lotus or circle, described about its middle chamber. Then he should fumigate the linen with the fumes of burnt Catechu wood, and hold under his feet, at the time, a piece of Bhurja bark, whereby he would be able to charm the three worlds with their inmates within seven days of practising such an incantation. In the alternative, the name of one's antagonist should be written at the centre of the lotus-shaped mystic diagram, provided with twelve petals and marked with the impressions of thunderbolts (and the letters of the Sada-Shiva-Mantra, and the necessary incantation should be susequently practised thereon, whereby the moving tongue of an accuser, would be paralysed, the lifted arm of an aggressor would be held spell-bound in the air, and the movements of an invading army, would be retarded. The same incantation may be practised by writing the name of the antagonist in pasted turmeric, either on a slab of stone, or on the rim of the sacrificial fire-pit (9-12).

The intelligent votary should write the name of his enemy in blood and poison, on a piece of deadman's rag picked up from a cremation ground, where the incantation should be practised, with the help of the hexagonal mystic diagram, held sacred to the goddess of the above-said Prastara, and bedecked with the mark of Danda, and written all over with the Shakti-Mantra, by which the enemy would meet his doom in no time, The same incantation, practised by writing the name of one's royal enemy on the blade of the discus, would be followed by political revolutions in his kingdom, which would ultimately bring about his death and ruin. The same incantation, practised by writing the name of one's enemy with the ashes, collected from a cremation ground, and on the blade of a sword, and vitalised by throwing charmed and charred remains of a human body over it, should be deemed as the most powerful agent in bringing about the death of one's enemy, and in creating dissensions in his camp. The present incantation, is sure to be crowned with the acquisition of a kingdom, within seven days of its practice (13-17).

The Mantras known as the Netras and the Tarakas, should be used in incantations practised for the prosperity and general welfare of a person. Such an incantation is known as the Dahanadi-Prayoga, and is potent enough to captivate even the mind of a Shakini. The mystic diagram, containing the Varuni-Mantra at its centre, and coupled with the one sacred to the god Vakratunda, should be deemed as a safe and certain cure for all sorts of epidermic diseases such as Leprosy, etc. The same diagram, containing the Karali-Mantra at its beginning, centre and the end, should be deemed as the breaker of all fetters, and a man wearing such a Yantram, is sure to be released from all places of incarceration. The votary should not divulge his own secret Mantra, even if the god Shiva himself would try to wrench it out of him. A rite of Nyasa performed with the Varuna-Mantras, is a positive cure for all sorts of cough and febrile distempers. A mystic Yantram, containing the Soumya-Mantras at the centre and the end, imparts greater weight to one's body, while the one containing the same Mantra at its beginning, middle and end, makes it light as a feather (18-21).

The abovesaid mystic diagram, bedecked with the marks of thunder-bolt, delineated in Rochona on a piece of Bhurja bark, and put in an amulet of gold, should be worn round the arm, by which all evils that would otherwise have invaded the body, would be averted. Such an amulet is a safe-guard against death, brings good luck to the wearer, and prevents the recrudescence of all evils and impediments. The wearer of such an amulet, is sure to return victorious from a battle, or from a gambling table, and a barren woman wearing such a one, is sure to be big with child in no distant time. Such an amulet should be looked upon as nothing short of the mystical gem known by the name of Chintamani. The Mantra, running as Streem, Kshem, Hum, Fut, should be repeated a hundred thousand times, whereby the repeater would conquer the dominion of a foreign king, and win the sovereignty of the world (22-25).

XXX

THE MANTRAS FOR THE GODDESS TVARITA

SAID THE GOD OF FIRE:—

Om, Hrum, Khe, Chhe, Ksha, Strim, Hrum, Kshe, Hreem, Fut, Obeisance to the goddess Tvarita. The goddess should be contemplated as possessed of two or four pairs of hands, and should be duly worshipped after having performed the rite of Naysa. The regent of universal receptivity (Adhara Shakti), as well as the lotus-cushion of the goddess, and her divine lion, should be worshipped in succession, and the rite of Sadanganyasa should be subsequently performed. The goddess, Gayatri should be worshipped at the eastern petal of the mystic lotus, and the attendant divinities of the goddess, such as Hunkara, Khechari, Chanda, Chhedini, Kshepeni, Kshemankari and Futkari, should be worshipped at the central part of the mystic diagram, by exhibiting the Pranita-Madras. The two hand-maids of the goddess, known as Jaya and Vijaya, should be worshipped at the door of the diagram, the Kinkaras having been worshipped in their front (1-3).

Subsequent to that, oblations of sesamum should be cast into the sacrificial fire by repeating the Vyahriti-Mantras, by which the votary would be able to obtain all he would ask for. Libations of clarified butter, should be poured on the fire, in honour of each of the undermentioned snake ornaments of the goddess, as follows:— Oblations with obeisance (Namah) Svaha to the primeval Hydra (Ananta), oblation with

Sacred words of Power

obeisance (Namah Svadha) to Kulika, oblation with obeisance (Svaha) to Vasukiraja. Oblation with obeisance (Vousht) to Shankhapala. Oblation with obeisance (Vashat) to Takshaka. Oblation with obeisance (Namas) to Maha-Padma. Oblation with obeisance (Svaha) to the serpent Karkata. Oblation with obeisance (Fut) to the serpent, Padma.

After that, the votary should lay down the diagram of in cantation, known as the Nigraha Chakra, and which consists of eighty-one terms, either on a piece of Bhurja bark, or on a stone slab, or on a piece of prepared canvas, or on a piece of linen, or he should curve it into the bough of a Vata tree. The name of the enemy, or the antagonist, should be written in the middle chamber of the diagram, or in those occupying its four cardinal points, in case where it would be delineated on a piece of prepared canvas. The Mantra, which should be recited in connection with the present incantation, runs as, Om, Hreem, Kshum, set down and set down the four thorns and draw close the veil of the night of death (4-8).

The mystic verse which should be written within the diagram of spell, and beyond the border of which the region of Pluto should be imagined as lying with all its horrors and monstrosities, runs as follows:-

Kalinara-ranalika-neena, Moksha Kshamonanee.
Mamodita Tadomoma Rakshatasva Svatakshara,
Yamapatha thapamaya Matha motha-thamothama.
Vamobhuri ribhumova tha tha rishva Shvari tha tha.

Water sprinkled over this region of Pluto, and consecrated with the Vam-, Tam- Mantras, should be deemed as the harbinger of death.

The verse should be written with a pen of crow's

quill, and in a composition made of collyrium, the gum of a Nimva tree, poison, and the marrow and blood of a human victim. A cremation ground, or a crossing of four roads, should be the place where the spell should be secretly practised. The charm should be either placed underneath a pitcher, or deposited inside an anthill, or should be hung on the bough of a Vibhitaka tree. The spell, in question, should be looked upon as the destroyer of one's opponents of all denominations (9-12).

Now I shall deal with the charm, which would counteract the baneful effects of the one described [in the preceding paragraph), and which is known as the circle of grace. (Anugraha Chakram). Both the spell, and its constituent verses, should be either written on a white leaf, or on a piece of Bhurja bark, and in a solution of shellac or saffron, or in sandal or chalk paste, as might be available. The Om Junsa Mantra should be written within the central chamber of the diagram, and in the left one counted from the east, and along its boundary walls, as well as on its ground plane, and also in the chamber at its west. The Mantras, known as Lakshmi Sloka (Shri Sukta) should be written all round the diagram, in the direction of south-east to the south-west. Then the mystic verses running as-

Sreeh Sāmayā Yāmasā Shreeh Sānon Yājne Jneyānonsā
Māyā Lilā Lālee Yāmā Yājne Nalee Leena Jneyā.

The abovesaid lotus circle, should be worshipped in the middle of a lotus flower. Such an incantation is a safeguard against death, and should be regarded as the greatest of all peace-giving rites, and also as a grantor of the highest fortune (13-17).

In dreadful incantations, the mystic chamber is to be divided into eleven (Rudra) chambers. The Vijas beginning with Om, and ending with Hung Fut, should be written in chambers at both the extremities of the diagram, the Adivarnas having been inserted in their middle. The Vidya varnas, ending with the Vasat-Vija, should be inserted below the line of the abovesaid Mantras, and below them should be written the Vijas, considered as Pratyangis to those mentioned in the preceding line. Such a diagram should be looked upon as the most powerful agent in bringing about the realisation of one's all desires. The circles of grace and oppression (Nigraha-nugraha Chakras), should be written with the eighty-one terms, mentioned above, and respectively held sacred to them. The Mantra, running as Kreem Sah Hum Fut, and known as the Amriti Vidya (incantation of reviving life), should be surrounded with three circular chains of the Hrung-Vijas. Such an incantation repeated by depositing the mystic diagram in a water-pitcher, is sure to kill all the enemies of the votary, and to confer upon him all sorts of boon. Being whispered into his ear, the incantation is sure to destroy all venom in a person, bitten by a venomous snake or animal, or exhibiting symptoms of malicious poisoning (18-23).

XXXI

THE MANTRAS FOR REALISING ONE'S ALL DESIRES

SAID THE GOD OF FIRE:–

The Mantra which begins with the Hung Vija,

and runs as Hung Khi, Chhi, Ksha, Streem Hung (*sic*), Kshi, Fut, should be deemed as the realiser of one's all desires, and an efficacious eliminator of all venom or poison from the human system. The Mantra running as Om, Kshi Chhe, should be used in reviving a person bitter by a deadly snake. The Mantra, running as Om, Hrim, Ke, Ksha, should be used in incantations, practised for neutralising the effects of poison, or for the purpose of bringing discomfiture of one's enemies. The Mantra, running as Streem, Hum, Fut, should be used in charms, possessed of the virtue of curing distempers due to one's sinful conduct; while the Mantras, Khi, Chha, should be deemed as the removers of all impediments to one's success. The Mantra, running as Hrum, Streem, Om, should be recited in charms, practised for winning the affection of a woman, while the Mantra, running as Khe, Streem, Khe, should be used in spells brewed for the death of an enemy, who has nearly gone through the natural term of his life. The Mantras, running as Ksha, Stree, Kshah, should be used in spells of victory and subjugation. Aim, Hrum, Shreem, Sphem, Kaim, Kshoum, O thou goddess Amvica (mother) Kuvjika, Sphem, Om, Bham, Tam, bring (such and a such person) under my control. Obeisance to thee, O thou dreadful mouthed one, Vram, Vreem, Kili, Kili, Vichcha, Sphoum, Haim, Sphrum, Shreem, Hreem, Aim Shreem. These Mantras, sacred tc the goddess Kuvjika, should be deemed as possessed of the virtue of imparting all sorts of boon. Now I shall disclose to you the Mantras which are held sacred to the god Isha (Shiva), and which were formerly revealed to the god Skanda (1-5).

XXXII

THE PRASADA MANTRA OF SHIVA

THE GOD SAID:—

O Guha, the Mantra sacred to the god Shiva, and known as the Prasada (Hroum), admits of a division into eight different classes, such as the Sakala (with the phases of beatitude), Niskala (without the phase of beatitude), Shunyam (the Mantra of absolute vacuum), Svamalankritam (adorned by his self), Kshapanam (Mantra of emanation), Kshayani (the Mantra of dissolution), and Kantoshtam. The letters of the alphabet required in writing the term Sadashiva should be deemed as the fountain source from which all sorts of success regarding penances and austerities, do emanate (1-2).

The rite of Nyasa in connection with the Mantra, should be performed by imagining the effulgent images of all the letters of the alphabet from A to Ksha, as located in the different parts of the body, together with the images of the following manifestations of Shiva, who are their respective tutelary divinities. The gods that preside over each of the letters are, Kamadeva, Shikhandi, Ganesha, Kala, Shankara, Ekanetra, Dvinetra, Trishikha, Dirgha-Vahuka, Ekapada, Ardha-Chandra, Valapa, Yoginipriya, Shakitishvara, Mahagranthi, Tarpaka, Sthanu, Dauntura, Nidhisha, Nandi, Padma, Shakunipriya, Mukhavimva, Bheeshana, Kritanta, Prana, Tejashvi, Shakra, Udadhi, Shrikantha, Sinha, Shashanka, Vishvarupa, Ksha, and Narasinha (3-8).

Then the rite of Pancha-Murti Nyasa, should be

performed as follows:—Houm, obeisance to the god Ishana located in my brain. Hem, obeisance to the Tatpurusha manifestation of the god. Hum, obeisance to Aghora, permeating the region of my heart, Hem, obeisance to Vamadeva, situated at the region of my arms, and Ham, obeisance to the Sadyojata manifestation of the god, permeating the region of my legs. All the Mantras, should be preceded by the Pranava, which should end with the name of each of the gods invoked in the dative case ending with the term Namas (obeisance) appended thereto (9-11).

Then the rite of Karanganyasa should be performed by appending the terms of obeisance, such as Namas, Svaha, Vasht, Hum, Fut, and Voushat to each of the proper Mantras, enjoined to be repeated on those occasions, together with the names of the different manifestations of the god, such as Sadyojata, Ishvara, etc., who are the regents of those parts of the human body.

Then the rite of subsequent Nyasa, should be performed with the comoponent letters of the Shiva Mantra, as follows:—Om obeisance to the heart, Nam obeisance to the head, Mam obeisance to the tuft of hair on the crown, Shim obeisance to the armour, Vam, obei5ance to the three eyes, and Yam obeisance to the weapon (12-17).

Then the Vija-Mantras, known as the Shikhas, coupled with the phonetic symbol of the crescent and followed by the term of obeisance, Fut, should be looked upon as no less than the mighty rident (Pashupata) of Shiva, and as the scourge of all evildoers. I have finished saying all about the Sakala Mantras, sacred to the god Shiva, now hear me discourse on those which pass by the denomination of the Nishkalas.

The Nishkala, or the Panchanga Mantras, sacred to Shiva, consist of the Vijas known as the Oushadha, Vishvarupa, Rudra, Surya, and the half-moon, coupled with the Nada Mantra, Om. A man, by repeating these Mantras, becomes entitled to all the pleasures of this life, and to salvation in the next (18-21).

The Mantras, which are known as the Shunyas, consist of the Vijas, known as the Anshumana, preceded and followed by the one of the Vishvarupa class, and divested of those which are grouped under the category of the Bramhangas. The Mantra should he made use of by boys and dull persons in general, whereby all impediments to their acquisition of knowledge, would be removed.

The Mantra known as the Kaladhya, consists of the Vijas known as the Anshumana, coupled with the Vishvarupam placed over the one known as the Uhaka. All the essential rites of worship, should be conducted in the same way, as laid down in a worship with the Sakala Mantras.

The Mantras known as the Svamalankritam, should consist of the Vijas known as the Narasinha, coupled with the Kritanta, and followed by the Anshuman, coupled with the one of Uhaka class. The rite of Nyasa in connection with the Mantra, should be performed with the Mantra, composed of the half moon, the Pranava, the Bramha, the Vishnu, the Udadhi, and the Narasinha Vijas, all other rites being done as in the preceding instances (22-26).

Then the Oja Vijas should be first coupled with

those known as the Anshumats, and which should be followed by the Anshumats coupled in their turn with the Anshus. The third Vija, should consist of those known as the Anshumana and the Ishvara, and the Mantra, thus framed, should be deemed as the grantor of salvation to its votary. The next Mantra should be composed in the following order:—First the Vija known as the Uhaka, should be written, coupled with an Anshu, which should be followed in due succession by a Varuna, Prana, Tejasha and a Kritanta Vija. The seventh Varna, should consist of the Anshumana, the Uhaka, the Prana, the Padma, the Indu, and the Nandisha Vijas, followed by the one of Ekapadadarik.

The Mantras, known as the Kshapana, should consist of these ten Vijas, from the beginning. The third, fifth and the seventh feet of the Mantra, should respectively consist of Mantras, numbering half as much. The ninth foot, should consist of the Vija, held sacred to the Sadyojata manifestation of the god, while the second foot, should consist of the Hrid-Mantras. The Mantras, consisting of the abovesaid ten Vijas, should end with the Fut, and which should be considered as the Astra-Mantra in the present case (27-31).

The rites of the Anganyasa in connection with the preceding Mantra, should be performed by appending the term Namas to the names of the eight Vidyeshvaras, such as Ananta, Isha, Sukshma, Shivottama, Ekamurti, Ekarupa, or Trimurti, Shrikantha and Shikhandi. The images of the manifestations of the god counted from that of Shikhandi to that of Ananta, should be considered as the images of the regents of the Mantra (32-34).

XXXIII

THE SAME MANTRA (CONTINUED)

THE GOD SAID:—

Place the Vishvarupa-Vija on the one known as the Tejasha, place the Narasinha Vija below that, and the Pranava-Mantra below that, and the Uhaka-Vija below that and the Anshumana-Vija below that, and below that the Hakara and the Pranava. The first four letters should end with the term Namas, and the Brahmangas, should be constructed as laid down in the preceding chapter (1-3).

First, take out the Pranava-Vija from the row constructed as above, by the process of elimination and coupling, known as the Mantroddhara, and then meditate upon the self of the god as a dreadful luminosity. Then divide the term Chata into two different parts, the term Daha in two, as well as the terms "Vama" and Ghata," and append thereto the terms Hung Fut. The Mantra thus framed, should be considered as the Astra-Mantra sacred to the Aghore manifestation of the god. Now I shall disclose to you the Gayatri Mantra, which is sacred to the same divinity, and which runs as follows:—We know the true self of the god Mahesha, who is the real and underlying substratum of the universe. We meditate on the divine self of the Supreme god (Maha deva), and may the blissful one (Shiva) lead our mind to that. This Gayatri grants all boons to her votaries (4-7).

The mystic diagram, should be divided into twelve rectilinear chambers, and the divinities, such as, Gana and Shree, should worshipped to the east of a quarter part of the entire figure. The worship should be made with a view to ensure the success of a mission, and by a person, before starting out on the same. A triangle should be inscribed within the mystic quadrilateral figure, and a lotus with three rows of petals should be drawn within the former. On the centre of the lotus steps and causeways, should be delineated, upon which the platform (Vedi), should be constructed to the height of a Bhaga only. The Mandala, thus constructed, should be furnished with doors and windows, with a lotus flower delineated at its centre. Such a Mandala, should be looked upon as a safeguard against all sorts of harms and evils that would otherwise have befallen the performer of the worship (8-11).

The lotus at the centre of the platform, should be coloured dark red, as well as the one, enclosing it within its circumference. The cause-ways should be coloured white, while the doors may be painted in any colour the votary would like. The petals, as well as the polens of the lotus, should be coloured yellow. The present Mandalam is named as the Vighnamardham (the remover of all impediments), on which the worship, should be commenced by making offerings to the god Ganapati. Then the gods, such as Indra, etc., should be worshipped by repeating the Tapturusha Mantra preceded by "Om" and followed by the term Namas (12-14).

Then the gods, such as Gaja, Gaja-Shirsha, Gangeya, Gana-nayaka, Triaravarta, Gaga, Naga and Gopati, should be worshipped on the eastern step of the Mandalam. Then the twelve gods, such as Vichitransha, Mahakaya, (the big-bodied one), Lamvoshtha (the god with the protruding lower lip), Lamvakarna (the long.eared one), Lamvodara (the big-bellied one), Mahabhaga (the generous-hearted one), Vikrita (the perverted one), Parvatipriya (the beloved of the daughter of the mountain), Bhayavaha (the one portending evil), Bhadra (the gentle one), Bhagana, and Bhayasudana (the remover of all dangers), should be worshipped on the ten steps of the Mandalam. The god Devatrasa (the terror of the celestials), should be worshipped in the west.

Subsequent to that, the gods Mahanada (the god of dreadful roar), Bhasvara (the effulgent one), Vighnaraja (the king of impediments), Ganadhipa (the lord of the Ganas), Udhbhata (the great sun), Svanabha (the self-originating one), Chanda (the irascible one), Mahashanda (all the powerful one), and Bhimaka (the dreadful one), should be worshipped in succession. The deities, such as Bramheshvara, Vrajhya, as well as the regents of the intellectual faculties, together with the principles of merging, both partial and absolute, and the gods such as Loulya (the greedy one), Vatsala (the affectionate one), Vikarna (the carless one), Manmatha (the agitator of the mind), Madhusuda, (the destroyer of Madhu), Sundara (the god of beauty), Bhavapusta (the one feeding on the sentiments), Kritanta (the god of death), Kaladanda (the measurer of eternal time), should be worshipped in the north of the Mandala, together with the sacrificial pitcher as described before (15-20).

The Mantra, sacred to the god, should be repeated ten thousand times at the close of the worship, and libations numbering a tenth part thereof, should be poured on the sacrificial fire, kindled on the occasion. Ten libations should be subsequently poured on the fire, by way of completing the ceremony, after which the final libation should be cast; and the worship should be terminated by ten times repeating the Mantra. The rite of Abhisheka should be performed subsequently, whereby the votary would attain all he would set his heart upon, and become the possessor of horses, elephants, and proprietary rights in real property (21-22).

XXXIV

THE CEREMONY OF ASTRA-YAJNAM

THE GOD SAID:-

The ceremony, known as the Astri Yajna, should be performed in all rites undertaken for ensuring worldly success. The weapons, sacred to the god Shiva should be worshipped at the centre, while the weapons, such as the Vajra, etc., should be worshipped in the different directions of the Mandala, commencing from the east. The five discuses, and the ten arms of the god, should be worshipped with a view to ensure success in battle. The planets should be worshipped in connection with the ceremony, whereby they would exert the same blissful influence, as they do when they are in the eleventh sign from that of one's nativity (1-3).

Now I shall deal with the rite of Astra Shanti, by which physical disturbances are quelled, epidemics

Sacred words of Power

are subsided, diseases, incidental to the malign influences of the baneful planets, are cured, and the enemies of the performer are annihilated. The Mantra, sacred to the Aghora manifestation of the god, and which is an infallible remedy for all diseases which owe their origin to the baneful influences of the Vinayakas, should be repeated, a hundred thousand times, in the beginning of the ceremony, whereby the evil influences of the planets would be removed. In cases of disturbances in Nature, libations, containing seeds of sesamum, and numbering a hundred thousand in all, should be poured on the fire, in succession, while phenomena portending evil, and restricting themselves to the sky, would vanish at the performance (of a Homa) consisting of libations, numbering half as much as in the preceding instance. Similarly, a hundred thousand libations of clarified cow-butter, poured on the fire, would quell all physical disturbances, which are peculiar to the earth. A rite of Homa, performed with libations of scented gum resin soaked in clarified cow-butter, should be deemed as the pacifier of all disturbances, whether physical or political. A rite of Homa, performed with libations of clarified cow-butter, containing grains of sun-dried, rice and bunches of Durva grass, should be deemed as an infallible remedy for all sorts of bodily distempers. A thousand libations of clarified cow-butter, would undoubtedly neutralise the ill effects of bad dreams, dreamt in the night. Likewise a ten thousand libations of clarified butter, containing the Java flowers, would propitiate the hostile planets and asterisms, whereas the same number of libations of clarified cow-butter, would cure all diseases that are incidental to the evil influences of the Vinayakas, and the malignant spirits. A Homa, performed with a ten thousand oblations of scented gum resin, would cleanse a spirit possessed by ghosts, and Vetalas, and a like ceremony should be gone through, on the occasion of a sudden falling off of a tree, of the class known as the Maha-Vrikshas, or of a perching down of a Vyala-Kanka on one's house-top (4-9).

Libations, consisting of clarified cow-butter, containing grains of sun-dried rice and bunches of Durva grass, should be poured on the sacrificial fire by a person, before entering a virgin forest. Libations, consisting of clarified cow-butter and the seeds of sesamum, remove all evils portended by earthquakes and meteor-falls. A ten thousand oblations of scented gum resin, would neutralise the ill effects of a tree, shedding blood, while a similar rite should be performed on the occasion of a tree blossoming, or bearing fruits in an improper season, or at the breaking out of an epidemic or of a political revolution. Similarly, a fifty thousand libations, consisting of sesamum seeds and clarified cow-butter, would stamp out an epidemic affecting the bipeds only, whereas the ceremony should be repeated at the breaking out of a pestilential disease, or on the occasion of an elephantess developing a pair of tusks, and portending evil to the state. The evil consequences of an elephantess, exuding serum from her temple, would be warded off by a Homa of ten thousand libations, whereas an epidemic of miscarriages of the womb, or of deaths of new-born infants in a community, would prove amenable to a similar Homa, consisting of as many libations (10-13).

Evil omens seen, by a person about to start on a

journey, should be atoned for by a performance of a Homa of ten thousand libations, whereas the libations should consist of sesamum and clarified cow-butter, and number one hundred thousand in all religious ceremonies, undertaken with a view to confer the highest supernatural powers on the votary, the libations respectively numbering a half and a quarter thereof as the attributes (Siddhis), would belong to the middling and the lowest class. An equal number of Japas and Homas, should be performed for victory in battle. A votary should repeat the Aghorastra-Mantra, after having performed the rite of Nyasa, and also after having meditated on the Panchasya (five-faced) manifestation of that divinity (14-15).

XXXV

THE BLISS OF THE SAME MANTRA

THE GOD SAID:-

Now I shall describe the rites of Japa and blissfulness, which are to be performed by repeating the Astra-mantra, known as the Pashupata. The component terms of the Mantra, should be repeated by appending the term "Fut" to each of them. The Mantra runs as follows:-

"Om obeisance to the God, the great Pashupata, who is possessed of matchless strength, prowess, and glory, and whose face is shining with fifteen eyes-obeisance to the god, who assumes varied forms, and is armed with various sorts of weapons and whose body, sable like pasted lamblack, is enlivened with jets of blood, and who is fond of the company of ghosts and Vetalas that frequent the cremation grounds. [Obeisance to] the remover of all impediments, to the grantor of all boons and successes in life, and to him who is always kind and benignantly disposed to his votaries. [Obeisance to] the god who is possessed of innumerable hands, feet, and mouths, to the perfected success, to the terror of all Vetalas, to the one who creates sorrow in the hearts of the Shakinis, to the healer of all diseases, to the purifier of all sinful souls, to the one, whose three eyes are the Sun, the Moon, and the fire,- to the phylactery sacred to the god Vishnu, to the wielder of swords and thunderbolts, to the wielder of the club of death and the trident of Varuna, to the trident of Rudra, to the one with the burning tongue, to the piercer of all diseases, to the oppressor of malignant planets, and to the annihilator of the whole race of malicious serpents. Om, obeisance to the black and the yellow one. Fut (obeisance) to Humkarastra. Fut to the wielder of thunderbolts. Fut to the goddess of energy. Fut, to the club. Fut to the god of death. Fut to the sword. Fut to the sword. Fut to the god Nairita. Fut to the god of ocean (Varuna). Fut to the noose. Fut to the banner. Fut to the mace. Fut to the god of wealth. Fut to the trident. Fut to the club. Fut to the discus. Fut to the lotus. Fut to the serpent weapon. Fut to the weapon Khetaka. Fut to the weapon Munda. Fut to the mace. Fut to the weapon Kankala. Fut to the weapon Pichhika. Fut to the weapon Kshurika (razor). Fut to the weapon Bramhastra. Fut to the weapon of Shakti. Fut to the weapon sacred to the Ganas. Fut to the weapon Pilipichhi. Fut to the weapon, sacred to the Gandharvas. Fut to the weapon of the Murva. Fut to the weapon known as the Dakshina.

Fut to the weapon, called the Vama. Fut to the weapon, known as the Paschima. Fut to the weapon, known as the Mantrastra. Fut to the weapon of the Shakinis. Fut to the weapons of the Yoginis. Fut to the club. Fut to the great club. Fut to the weapons of the Nagas. Fut to the weapon of the mighty Shiva. Fut to the weapon of the god Ishana. Fut to the weapon of the god Purusha. Fut to the weapon of Aghora. Fut to the weapon of Sadyojata. Fut to the weapon of the Hridaya. Fut to the Mahastra. Fut to the weapon of Garuda. Fut to the weapon of Rakshasa. Fut to the weapon of the Danavas. Fut to the weapon sacred to the Nrisinha manifestation of Vishnu. Fut to the weapon sacred to the god Tvastra. Fut to all the weapons.

Nah Fut, Vah Fut, Pah Fut, Phah Fut, Mah Fut, Shree Fut, Pheh Fut, Kram Fut, Krom Fut, Bhuh Fut, Bhuva Fut, Sva Fut, Fut to the region Maha, Fut to the region Jana. Fut to the region Tapas. Fut to all the regions. Fut to all the nether regions. Fut to all the fundamental principles of the universe. Fut to all the principles of vitality. Fut to all the the veins and arteries. Fut to all the causes. Fut to all the gods. Kreem Fut, Hreem Fut, Shreem Fut, Hum Fut, Srum Fut, Svam Fut, Lam Fut. Fut to the spirit of indifference to the concerns of life. Fut to the weapon of illusion. Fut to the weapon, which is composed of the principle symbolised by the Mantra Hum. Fut to the Weapon-Mantra, sacred to the god of day. Fut to the Weapon-Mantra, sacred to the Moon-god. Fut to the weapon, sacred to the god, who is the remover of all impediments. Goum, Goum Fut. Khrom Khoum. Fut, Hroum, Houm Fut. Cause (him) to roam and roam about, Fut. Eclipse and Eclipse [his soul], lift and lift (him) by the heel. Fut, threaten and threaten (him). Fut, Fut, revive and revive. Disperse and disperse, Fut. Destroy and destroy all sins, Fut (1).

A single repetition of the abovesaid Mantra, would purge a man of all sins committed by him in life, whereas a hundred recitation would quell all disturbances in his country, and grant him victory in war. The Homa in connection with the ceremony, should consist of libations of clarified cow-butter saturated with the scented gum resin, whereby the most utopian schemes of its performer, would be realised. A single repetition of this Astra-Pashupata-Mantra, should be deemed as the best of all peace-giving rites (2-3).

XXXVI

THE MANTRA FOR CURING DISEASES AND WARDING OFF DEATH

THE GOD SAID:—

O thou six-faced one, the Mantra running as Om, Hrum, Hansa, is possessed of the virtue of curing diseases and warding off death. The Homa, in connection with the Mantra, should be performed by pouring out a hundred thousand libations of clarifed butter, containing bunches of Durva-grass, on the fire, whereby the health and general peace of the life of the performer would be increased. In the alternative, weird and portentious phenomena occurring in the sky or in the earth, or those which owe their origin to the agency of the gods, as well as auguries of evil omen, such as the unnatural blossoming of trees, etc., should be atoned for by repetitions of such Mantras as the Pranavas, the Maya, etc., (1-2).

Om obeisance to the goddess Ganga. O thou Kali, Kali, O thou supreme Kali, O thou Supreme Kali, O thou, who livest on flesh and blood, and whose face, sable as that of the night, is blazoned by streaks of blood, bring all men under my control, obeisance Om. The Mantra should be repeated a hundred thousand times, and libations, numbering a tenth part thereof, should be poured on the fire. A man by repeating the Mantra, and doing the necessary Homa, would subjugate the mind of the lord of the celestials, not to speak of men. By means of the above-said Mantra, a votary would be able to remain invisible to all men. It is the best of all charms, and is potent enough to bring one's enemies under control, and to paralyse all their intellectula faculties. The Mantra, seven times repeated, should be looked upon as same as the celestial milch-cow (Kama-Dhenu (3-5).

Now I shall narrate to you the king of the Mantras, the safeguard against depredations by thieves and robbers. In peril, and during the prevalence of pestilential epidemics, the Mantra, worshipped by the mighty Shiva, should be repeated a hundred thousand times, and libations numbering a tenth part thereof, should be poured on the fire.

Now hear me narrate the Mantra of universal succour, and which runs as:—Om, O thou, who dost wield a trident, come and come, preserve me with the truths that form the essences of the gods Brahma, Vishnu, and Rudra, Om, obeisance to the god Vacheshvara (Svaha).

Since the goddess succours men from distressed conditions (Durgas), she is called Durga. The Mantra, sacred to the goddess, runs as follows:- Om, Chanda-Kapalini, dost thou gnash and gnash thy teeth. Fut, Hreem. Grains of rice, should be consecrated with the preceding Mantra, and should be given to the suspected thief for chewing. The innocence of the man would be established in the event of the ejected cud having retained its natural whiteness (6-8).

Om, O thou with a pair of burning eyes and the clotted and dark-brown hairs on whose head, burns with terrific fire. O thou stupefier and piercer of the three regions of beings, cut and cut, roam about and roam about, attract and attract, break and break, twist and twist, burn and burn, cook and cook, thus what Siddha-Rudra commands. I shall bring thee down even though thou be at this hour in the fields of Elysium, or in the region of the higher gods, or wantonly sporting on the summit of the mount of felicity. I make offerings to thee, dost thou accept them !

Thus having made offerings to the god Kshetrapala, the votary should practise the rite of Graha-Nyasa, whereby he would bring the whole world under his control. The enemies of such a person, would meet their doom, and his antagonists would be carried away in battle (9).

A man, having performed the rite of Nyasa with the Hansa-Vija, should procure three sorts of poison, and mix them up with the powders of the drugs, known as the Agaru, the Sandal, the Kushtha, the Saffron, the Nagakesharam, the Nakha, and the Devadaru, taken in equal parts, and made into a paste with honey. Then he should fumigate the clothes of an idol with the vapours thereof, whereby he would meet with good luck in quarrels, charms, and literary diseuisitions. The same fumigation should be consecrated withe Maya-Mantr,a where the object would be to win a bride. A Tilak mark made of Gorochana, Nagapushpa, Saffron, and Manahshila, and put on the forehead of a person, consecrated with the Hreem-Mantra, would act as an irresistible charm. Pulverised Shatavari, taken with milk, helps a man in begetting a male child, and the same result is also obtained by taking the powders of Nagakeshara boiled in clarified cow-butter, or the washings of Palasha seeds, simple and alone (10-14).

Om, rise and rise, O thou goddess Chamunda, overtake and overtake, charm and charm, such and such a person, and bring him under my control, obeisance (Svaha). The Mantra, which is infallible in its efficacy, should be repeated twenty six-times over a lump of clay brought from the bank of a river. An image should be made with that of the wished for lady. Her name should be written in the juice of the Unmatta plant on an Arka leaf, and the image should be placed thereon. Then the votary should pass water over the charm, and repeat the preceding Mantra, whereby he would have the lady drawn to his side.

Om, Kshum, Sah, Fut. This Mantra, known as the great Death-conquering one, should be made use of in Homas and chanted at regulated times, by which the health and beauty of the votary would be increased.

Om, Hansah, Hrum, Hum, Sa, Hrah, Soum. The Mantra consists of eight letters, and is known as the

Reviver of. life. The Mantra should be repeated with a view to obtain victory in war (15-17).

The god Ishana is the presiding divinity of all the Mantras, and is the lord of the Brahmanas, and of all the created beings. May the god Sada-Shiva confer eternal bliss on me.

Om, may I know the divine self of the god Tat-Purusha, may I meditate upon his divine self, and may Rudra lead it to dwell thereon. Om, obeisance to the Aghoras, to the Ghoras, to the Ghora-Ghoras, and to all the manifestations of Rudra, and on all sides.

Om, obeisance to Vamadeva. Obeisance to Jestha. Obeisance to Rudra. Obeisance to Kala. Obeisance to Kalavi karana. Obeisance to Valavikarana. Obeisance to Vala Pramathana. Obeisance to the controller of all created things and beings, and obeisance to the god who agitates the minds of all.

Now I shall narrate the Sadyojata-Mantra, which runs as follows:—Obeisance to Sadvojata Obeisance to the god of being. Obeisance to the god of eternal being. Be manifest in me, O thou god, who hast proceeded out of the eternal being, and dost control the process of infinite becoming.

Om, obeisance to the supreme soul, to the supreme one. Obeisance to the grantor of all desires, obeisance to the supreme god, obeisance to the god of self-communion, Obeisance to the god who proceeds out of the process of self-communion, obeisance to the doer of all, do and do and be manifest and be manifest, O thou, who dost control the process of eternal Becoming. Be propitiated, O thou

Vamadeva, the doer of all acts, the expiator of all sins, O thou, the ever blissful one. Obeisance to thee and obeisance.

The Hrid-Mantra in connection with the above, runs as follows:—Om Shivah, obeisance to Shiva. Om obeisance to the flaming energy situate in the region of my heart. The Shikha-Mantra, in connection with the present Nyasa, runs as Om, O thou supreme energy proceeding out of the divine essence of Shiva, O thou omniscient being, O thou lord of all, be evolved out, O thou matchless dreaded being, and O thou, who wearest long, brown and clotted locks on thy head. Obeisance to thee, O thou great armour, O thou who wieldst bolts of subtle thunder, and art equipped with nooses of lightning, and bows and arrows of the same fierce fluid, dost thou enter my body, and bind and bind, crumble down and crumble down, whirl and whirl round, and stupefy and stupefy the hearts of all malicious creatures. Stupefy and stupefy all malignant beings, Hum.

The present phylactery (Kavacham) consists of a hundred and five letters. The Astra-Mantra, sacred to the Aghora manifestation of the god, runs as:- Om obeisance to the dreadful energy (Ojas) of the god, permeating the region of my eyes. Om, be thou effulgent and effulgent, O thou whose essence is too subtle to be perceived by the senses. Let thy wrath and anger fill in this infinite space of the universe. Kill and kill, cut and cleave and vomit and vomit forth fatal fire. Hrung, Fut (18-20).

XXXVII

THE PEACE-GIVING RITE OF SHIVA-SHANTI

THE GOD SAID:—

Now I shall describe to you the peace giving rite known as the Shiva-Shanti, and the Mantra called the Aghorakalpa, which forms the pith and marrow of such a ceremony. The rite in question absolves even the killer of a Brahmana, of all sins incidental to such an act, is the abode of all the three sorts of penitential successes, and is the healer of all distempers that afflict the human flesh or mind. Phenomena that portend evil, are subsided under the pacifying influence of the ceremony, whether they appear in the sky or heaven, or are brought about by the direct intervention of the gods. Fatal influences of dreadful poison or malignant stars and spirits, are known to have yielded to its effect. The rite is the best atonement for all sins, is the most powerful agent in giving a better turn to one's fortune, and is the best dispeller of all gloom that hangs over the mind of a man (1-3).

The rite of Nyasa, in connection with the ceremony, should be performed, by mentally assigning the different parts of one's body to the Eknetra manifestation of the god, after which the votary, should meditate upon the divine self of the five-faced one. The faces of the god, should be contemplated white, in all religious ceremonies, undertaken with a view to confer peace and prosperity on a person, red or yellow in charms, brown in acts where the object would be stupefiction of one's intellectual faculties or organic functions, while they should be imagined

Sacred words of Power

dark black in fatal or maddening incantations. The faces should be imagined as burning with a twany or flaming hue in incantations of oblivion, or of attracting the mind of a man towards one's self. The Mantra consisting of thirty-two letters, should be first worshipped, and then repeated a thirty lakhs of time. Libations of clarified cow-butter, and numbering a tenth part of the latter, should be poured on the fire. Such libations consisting of the essence of gum-resin, and poured on the fire as stated in the preceding line, convert a novice into an adept in the spiritual mysteries, and help him in attaining whatever he sets his mind upon. The Aghora-Mantra grants both worldly good and salvation of the soul, and there is no other Mantra which can vie with it in that respect. By repeating it, a man, who is not an ascetic, acquires the fullest merit of asceticism, and a man who has never gone through the vow of religious ablution, becomes a Snataka (a religious bather) in every acceptance of the term. The Aghora, and the Aghora-astra, Mantras are the two kings of the Mantras. The rites of Homa, Japa, and worship in connection with the Mantra, if duly performed, would enable a man to annihilate his enemy's army in battle (4-8).

Now I shall describe the ever blissful rite of Rudra-Shanti, which confers upon its performers, whatever he has an eye to. Barren women become mothers, malignant planets become friendly, and diseases become scarce under the benign influence of the present ceremony. Famine forsakes a country, pestilence never visits its shores, and evil dreams never oppress the sleep of its inmates, where the ceremony in question is performed. Kingdoms and armies own him as their lord, who performs it, and his enemies are overwhelmed with ruin. The rite should be undertaken when evil times would be prophesied by the unnatural blossoming of trees, or by inauspicious dreams in the night. The term Namas, should be appended to the Mantra in a worship, while it should terminate with a Svaha, a Vashat, and a Voushat respectively in rites of Homa, pacification and prosperity. The term "Cha" should be used in the second place, as illustrated in the following example:-

Om, obeisance to Rudra and (Cha) to thee. Om obeisance to the bull. Obeisance to the unemancipated one. Om, obeisance to the unborn one. Obeisance to the infinite personality, and (Cha) to the worshipful Ishana, the infinite prowess.

The following five manifestations of the god (Rudra), should be worshipped to the north of the mystic diagram as follows:—Obeisance to the one whose aspect is the universe. Obeisance to the dreadful one. Obeisance to the one of distorted features, and Om, obeisance to the one who knows no change. The worship should be conducted at the southern, and the south-western, points, of the mystic diagram in the principles of water and illusion.

Obeisance to the god Eka-Pingala, to Shveta Pingala, and to Krishna-Pingala. Obeisance to the god Madhu-Pingala, invoked in the principle of predestination. Obeisance to the eternal one, to the moist (compassionate) one, to the withered (merciless) one, and to the god Payogana, invoked in the principle of eternal time. Obeisance to the thousand-headed one, to the thousand-mouthed one, to the thousand-handed and thousand-footed divinity, and to the thousand-phallased one invoked in the southern petal of the lotus-shaped diagram (9-13).

Obeisance to the god with a single braid of clotted hair. Obeisance to the god with a couple braids of clotted hair. Obeisance to the god with three braids of clotted hair. Obeisance to Kara. Obeisance to Akara. Obeisance to Vashat-Kara, and lastly, obeisance to the six Rudras. O Guha, the offerings are to be made to the aforenamed divinities, invoked in the principle of dissolution, and supposed to be present at the south-eastern point of the mystic diagram.

Obeisance to the lord of the world. Obeisance to the lord of all the created beings. Obeisance to the goddess Uma and to the lord of eternal time. The offerings are to be made in the spiritual principle, presided over by the god Sadashiva, and supposed to have been invoked at the eastern petal of the mystic diagram (4).

Obeisance to the goddess Uma who assumes dreadful shapes. Om, come and come and hasten and hasten, O thou Rohini, who art but another manifestation of the god Rudra, the lord of the celestials. Kill and kill, burn and burn. Cook and cook. Trample down and trample down. Come and come, and hie thee and hie thee to the mission of the present rite of Rudra-Shanti. Obeisance to the black and brown coloured one, obeisance to the universal god who is the lord of the Akala Pishachas, as well. The god Maheshvara with his consort Uma should be worshipped in the spiritual principle sacred to Shiva, and invoked for permeating the polens of the lotus-shaped mystic diagram.

Om, obeisance to the spirit, filling in the space of the universal ether. Om obeisance to the god whose body is the infinite heaven. Om, obeisance to the all pervading Shiva, to the eternal lordless Shiva, who does not depend on any thing for his support.

The following seven terms are the epithets of the sky pervading Shiva, and offerings should be made, O Guha, by addressing each of these names, in the eastern petal of the mystic lotus. permeated with the spiritual principle, presided over by the god Sada-Shiva, as follows:—Om, obeisance to the eternal being who feeds upon the contemplation, and who is the eternal Yogin, and is eternally present in the circle of yoga. Om obeisance to Shiva, the five-faced one, the lord of all, the absolute subjectivity the chief of the Ishanas.

The following manifestations of the god, should be worshipped in the principle of Homa invoked in the south-eastern petal of the lotus diagram, and in the two principles of knowledge invoked in the one at the north:- Om obeisance and obeisance to the heart of the illusionless one, to the mystery of Vamadeva, and to the Sadyojata manifestation of the god. Om obeisance and obeisance to the mystery of all mysteries, to the preserver, to the deathless one, to the subject of all Yoga, and to the primal light.

The following manifestations of the god, should be worshipped in the principles of illusion and eternal time, respectively situate at the north-western, and the western, petals of the lotus:- Obeisance to the supreme god, to the conscious and unconscious one, to the sky-pervading one, and to the light of the first light.

Om, O thou deathless one, O thou Shiva who art born of death, O thou all, O thou supreme soul, O thou great god, O thou infinite energy, O thou, the lord -of good feelings, O thou, the presiding deity of all yoga, dost thou emancipate and emancipate our soul,—Om, O thou all, Om, O thou the lord and product of all becoming. Om, O thou who givest felicity to all creatures. This Mantra should be worshipped in the principles of fatality and subjective freedom, respectively invoked in the north-western, and northern, petals of the lotus.

Hie thee, and hie thee, O thou spirit who dwellest near all, and art worshipped by Bramha, Vishnu and Rudra, O thou who art above all hymns and worship, and dost witness all actions in the universe. Come and come, O thou, the sun, the fire, the knowledge, the sound, the subtle principle, come, O thou blissful one, the giver of all, and grantor of all, felicity. Om obeisance to Shiva, Om, obeisance. The worship should be made with the preceding Mantra in the principle of Nature, invoked in the north-eastern petal of the mystic diagram. The ceremony should be closed with the rites of necessary Homas and Japas, whereby all desires would be fulfilled, and all diseases incidental to the malign influences of planets, would be cured (15-17).

XXXVIII

THE METRE OF THE DIVINE GAYATRI

SAID THE GOD OF FIRE:-

In Prosody the metre known as the divine (Daivi) Gayatri, consists of a single syllable, the one, known as the Asuri (Demonic) Gayatri, consists of fifteen syllables, while the one, known as the Prajapatya, consists of eight syllables or varnas. The metre, as used in the Yajur Vedas, consists of six syllables, while the Samagas add two syllables more its foot. The metre, as used in the Rik Vedas, consists of eighteen syllables, while the chaunters of Saman, add two syllables more to its quarter, at will. Three syllables are usually over-allotted to the foot of a Rich, four to the foot of a Prajapati, and so on, while a syllable is always excluded from the foot of an Asuri (1-3).

The metres such as the Ushnika, the Anstupa, the Vrihati, the Pankti, the Tristupa, the Jagati, etc., are formed by combinations and permutations of the syllables allotted to the quarter of the original Gayatri,- syllables, which in groups of three, may count up to sixty-four in each quarter (4-5).

XXXIX

THE METRE JAGATI

Said the God of Fire:-

I have already dealt with the syllabic incidents which form the metre Gayatri, such terms as Yas, etc., occurring in its quarters, should be deemed as used simply with the object of making up the metre and saving the verse. The metre, known as the Jagati consists of twelve syllable, the Virat of ten, and the Tristubha of eleven syllables only. The metre Gayatri consists of a single quarter, or it may consist of three quarters or feet, of seven syllables each, or occasionally of four quarters, composed of seven letters in each. The metre Gayatri is formed as stated in the proceeding line. The metre Ati-Gayatri is composed of three quarters of six syllables each. The metre Vardhmana is composed of twenty-one syllables, and the Nagi of twenty-four. The metre Varahi is composed of twenty-seven syllables. The third metre consists of two or three quarters, according to the option of the versifier, each quarter being composed of twenty syllables of Trastupa (1-5).

The metre, known as tile Ushinka, consists of eight letters as often found in the Vedas. The metre, known as the Kukubhushnika, consists of three quarters of twenty-eight syllables. The quarters of a verse of the metre Pura-Ushnika follow the same rule as regards scanning, as the quarters of the Jagati, while the metre, known as the Paroshnika, consists of four quarters of seven syllables each. An Anustupa consists of four quarters of eight syllables each. The metre Vrihati consists of quarters of thirty-two syllables. Of the three Jagatas formed, form the original Gayatri, the second is called the Nanku-Sarini, which the third is called the Pathya. The Maha-Vrihatis are formed by the three Jagatas, as well as the Sato-Vrihati of Tandin. The metre Pankti consists of four quarters of forty syllables. The metres, which are but the modifications of the original Pankti, are the Satah-Pankti, the Prastara-Pankti, the Astara-Pankti, the Vistara-Pankti, the Sanstara-Pankti, etc. The metre Pathya consists of five Gayatris, and the Jagati of six. The other Vedic metres such as the Virat, the Svarat, the Shankumati, the Kukumvati, etc., will be dealt with later on (6-1 4).

The presiding deities of the metres, should be determined from their first quarters. The divinities, such as the Fire-God, the Sun, the Moon, the Jupiter, the Ocean-God and Indra, and the Vishvedevas, are the deities who are the regents of metres, belonging both to the Vedic and the secular literature. The Gamut of sound, such as the Sadaja, the Gandhara, the Madhyama, the Panchama, the Dhaivata and the Nishada, respectively belong to them. The white, the fawn, the brown, the black, the blue, and the red, are the colours which mark the complexions of the spirits of those metres. The spirit of the metre Gayatri is a gold complexioned one. The complexion of the spirits of different classes of Kritis are like that of Gorochona (yellow), while that of the spirit of the metre Jyotishmati is blue. The Gotras to which the different Vedic metres belong, are Agniveshya, Kashyapa, Goutama, Angirasa, Bhargava, Koushika and Vashishta (15-20).

XL

THE METRE UTKRITI

SAID THE GOD OF FIRE:—

The metre Utkriti consists of hundred and four syllables (*i.e.*, twenty-six syllables in each quarter). Thus by dropping four syllables as well as the prefixes Abhi, Sam, Vi, Am, Pra, etc., from them we get the metre Kriti, and the other classes of metres, such as the Kriti, the Ati-Dhriti, the Dhriti, the Atyasti, the Asti, the Ati-Shakvari, the Ati-Jagati, and the Jagati, and which are usually come across in secular literature. The metres, such as the Tristupa, the Pankti, the Vrihati, the Anustupa, and the Ushnika, etc., owe their origin to the Vedic Traistubha (1-3).

Sacred words of Power

The metres, such as the Gayatri, the Supratishta, the Pratishta, the Madhya, the Atyuktha, and the Uktha, are all convertible into one another, a preceding metre being converted into the succeeding one, simply by dropping a letter or a syllable. A Pada. (quarter) is the fourth part of a metrical stanza; and now I shall deal with the Ganas Chhandah (metre regulated by syllabic instant), and begin with the Arya.

The first and the third quarters of the metre respectively contain twelve syllabic instants of Matras, such as (first quarter) short, short-short, short-long (=2 short) short short-long, long) (third quarter) short, short-short, short, long, short, short,-short, short, long, (second quarter) consisting of eighteen syllabic instants (long, short, Short, long, long, short, long, short, long, long, long), and the fourth quarter consisting of fifteen syllabic instants, (as long, long, short, short, long, short, long, long). The metre Vipula should be scanned as follows:—The first quarter consisting of eighteen syllabic instants, such as (long, long, short, short, long, long, long, short, short, long, long. The second quarter consisting of twelve syllabic instants, such as (long, short, short, short, short, long, long, long), the third quarter consisting of fourteen syllabic instants such as (long, short, short, short, long, short, long, long, long.) The fourth quarter consisting of thirteen syllabic instants, such as (long, long, long, short, long, short, short, long). The metre Chapala consists of the following syllabic instants. First quarter of 12. S. I. (short, short, long, short, long short, long, long). Second quarter of 18 S. I. (short, long, short, long, long, short, long, short, long, long, long. Third quarter of 12 S. I. (long, long, short, long, short, long, long) and the fourth quarter of 15. S. I. (short, long, short, long, long, short long, long, long). The Mukha-Chapala consists of the following S. I. First quarter of 12 S. I. (long, short, short, short, long, short, long, long). Second, quarter of 18 S. I. (short, long, short, long, long, short, long, short, long, long, long), the third quarter of 12 S. I. (long, short, short, short, short, long, long, long). Fourth quarter of 15. S. I. (long, short, short, long, long, short, short, short, short, short, long). In the metre Chaplarya, the first half of the second quarter consists of syllabic incidents peculiar to the Jaghana-Chapala. A combination of these two classes of metres, gives rise to what is called the Maha-Chapala. The metre Aeya-Giti consists of the following syllabic incidents. First quarter of 12 S. I. (Long, long, long. short, short, short, short, long). Second quarter, of 20 S. I. (short, long, short, long, long, short, long, short, long, short, short, short, long, long). The third quarter of 12 S. I. (long, long, long, long, long, long), the fourth quarter of eighteen S. I. (long, long, long, long, short, long, short, short, short, long, short, long) (4-11).

In the metre Vaitalyum (sometimes treated as a Vritti) it is necessary that the syllabic incidents in the even quarter, should not be all composed of short syllables, or long syllables, and that the even syllabic instants in each quarter (the 2nd, 4th and 6th) should not be formed conjointly with the third, fifth and seventh. In the case of an Oupachhandasika, the rule is same as in the preceding instance, except that at the termination of each quarter, there should be a Ra-Gana and a Ya-Gana instead of a Ra-Gana, and a La and a Ga only. The quarters of a Patalika end with Bha, Ga and Ga, Ganas. The metres known as the Charu-Hasini, and Aparantika, fall to the class of Ayuk. The metre called the Matrasamana consists of four quarters, each of sixteen syllabic instants. The metre Vanavasika is but a modification of the preceding one, in which the ninth and the twelfth moments are formed by short syllables, and the fifteenth and the sixteenth by long ones, the rest being optional. Similarly the same metre is called the Chitra, if the fifth, eighth, and ninth, are formed by short syllables, and the fifteenth and the sixteenth by long ones.

In the Upa-Chitra, the fifth, the eighth, the ninth, and the tenth are short, and the fifteenth and the sixteenth are long, and if the fifth, eighth and twelfth are short, and the fifteenth and the sixteenth are long, and the rest indefinite, the metre is called the Vishloka. Sometimes two or more of these varieties combine to form a new metre (Padakulaka) which does not obey any other restriction save that each quarter would contain sixteen syllables (12-18).

XLI

MANTRA CURES (CURATIVE FORMULAS) OF SNAKE BITE AS NARRATED BY S'IVA

SUTA SAID:-

I will now describe the higly secret mantrams narrated by Shiva. His weapons are the noose, the bow, the discus, the club, the dart and Pattisha. Having used these weapons inspired with mantrams in a battle a king conquers his enemies. The mantram for purifying the mantans should be first written on a lotus petal. Om is the Brahma *Vijam*. Hrim is the Vishnu *Vijam*. These three Vijams should be assigned to the head of Shiva thrice in order.

Om, Hrim, Hrim.

Having taken up the dart in his hand he should whirl it in the sky. By seeing it all the evil stars and serpents are destroyed. Having held the smoky coloured bow by the hand a man should meditate on it in the sky. By it the wicked serpents, the evil stars, clouds and Rakshasas are destroyed. This mantram protects the three worlds, what to speak of the land of mortals?

Om, jum, Sam, Hum, Phat. Eight sticks of Catechu wood, inspired with mantrams, should be placed on the ground. That will prevent the falling of thunderbolt. The eight sticks should be inspired with great mantram described by Garuda. The ground should be dug twenty one times in the night. This will ward off the dangers proceeding from lightning, mouse, and thunder bolt.

The mantram is:—Hara, Kshara, amala, Vashat, added with Vindu Sadasiva.

Om, Hram, salutation unto Sadashiva.

He should then assign p*indu* (balls of rice) effulgent like Darimi flowers with the fore-finger. By seeing it the evil clouds, lightning and other enemies viz. the Rakshasas, goblins and female ghosts fly away into the ten quarters.

Om, Hrim, salutations unto Ganesha. Om, Hrim, salutation unto the chakra of Sthambhana.

Om, em, salutation unto the Damaras of the three worlds.

This *pinda* is called Bhairava which counteracts the effect of poison and the evil effects of the hostile planets. It protects the field and grinds the goblins and Rakshasas.

Om, Namas. Having meditated on the thunderbolt of his hand he should ward off the evil influence of wicked clouds and with Vajra Mudra all the ghosts, the enemies with poison. Om, Kshum, Namas. He should meditate on his left hand. It destroys all venomous creatures.

Om, Hram, Namas. The very recitation of this mantram destroys the evil colds and stars. Having meditated on death he should consume the universe with the destroying weapon.

Om, Kshma, Namas.

Meditating on Bhairava one should remove the evil influences of stars, goblins and poison.

Om lasat, jhvaksha Swāhā. This mantram destroys the enemies of the field *viz.*, the evil stars, goblins poison and birds.

Om Ksham Namas. The figure of a cistern should be drawn with blood and then the names of planets, should be written there.

Om, Mara, Mara, Maraya, Maraya Swāhā. Om, Hum, Phat, Swāhā.

The dart should be inspired mentally with eight hundred mantrams. It destroys all the enemies.

With higher energies the lower ones should be suppressed.1 Then the mantrams should be practised in *Puraka*2 and should be again well inspired in *Kumbhaka*. They should then be received with Pranava.

When the mantrams are thus properly received and used they yield fruts like servants.

XLII

ENUMERATION OF DIVERSE INCANTATIONS, MATRAS (NANA VIDYA)

VASUDEVA SAID:—

Om, there is a Gandharva, by name Vishwāvasu, the master of maidens. I will secure him for you. "Having begotten maidens. Unto Vishwavasu, Swāha." This is the recitation of the mantram for obtaining wives. I will describe the night of death.

Om, salutation unto the auspicious goddess, having ears like those of a bear and four arms. O thou having hairs, tied up! O thou, having three eyes! This is the night of death for men in the matter of feeding upon marrow and blood. May death approach such and such person who has come to the proper time. Ham, phat, kitt, kitt, burn, burn, flesh and blood, pacha, pacha, Rikshapatni (wife of the bear) Swahā. There is no restriction for the observance of lunar days, stars, or fasting.

A worshipper should rub his hands with blood and then take up all articles with them. Early in the morning he should recite the name of the phallic emblem and strike it with a mangoe leaf. Om, salutation unto all the weapons, so that, O Jambhani, O thou who charmest all, O thou who dost destroy all the enemies, protect me, such and such a person, from all fears and calamities, Swahā. On the destruction of Shukra, O Mahadeva, I described it which saves all the twice-born.

XLIII

THE HYMN TO NARASIMHA

SUTA SAID:—

O Shaunaka, now I shall narrate the hymn to Narasinha, as composed by Shiva. The Mātrikās of yore addressed the blissful one (Shankara) as follows:- we shall devour, O lord, all the demons and men, if you so permit us. The universe is from thee, O lord.

SHANKARA SAID:—O you goddesses, I think it is rather incumbent on you to preserve the inmates of the universe: banish, O goddesses, these cruel intentions from your minds.

SUTA SAID:—Even thus being addressed by Shankara, the ferocious Mātrikās paid no heed to his counsels and began to devour the universe with all its inmates, both mobile and immobile. The god Shiva meditated upon the form of Nrishinha while the Matrikas were engaged in devouring the universe. The endless and originless Shiva contemplated a form which inspired terror in the hearts of all creatures. The manes on his neck stood up erect on their ends. His dreadful teeth were illuminated with the lurid light of his lightning-tongue, which fearfully lolled out. His was a voice which resembled the roar of the seven oceans, agitated by the tornado of universal dissolution. He pulled aside the corners of his lips with the tips of his finger-nails, which were hard as thunder-bolts. His eyes had a glow, which resembled that of the summits of the mount Meru reflecting back the splendour of the rising sun. His body was like the summit of the Himalayas, illuminated with the reflected blaze of his diabolical teeth. The manes on his neck were burning, like the tongues of fire, with rage. He wore a crown of gold on his head and bracelets of gems round his wrists. Girdles composed of chains of gold decorated his waist, and the whole expanse of universe was illumined with the glow of his complexion, which was like the colour of a blue lotus. Ringlets of hairs grew on his body, and he wore a garland of beautiful and multi-coloured flowers. The god, thus meditated upon by Shankara, instantly appeared before him in this form, and Shankara propitiated this dreadful vision of Nrisinha.

SHANKARA SAID: Salutation unto thee, the lord of the universe. Thou hast assumed the form of Narasinha and bearest the entrails of the demon king on thy finger-nails. Obeisance to thee, the lotus-naveled one, whose complexion illumines the whole expanse of the universe. Obeisance to thee, the beautiful one, effulgent as a million suns, and whose voice is like the roar of the universal ocean of dissolution. I make obeisance to thee, who art dreaded by thousands of the lords of death, who bearest the strength of thousand Indras in thy limbs, whose riches exceed those of thousand of Kuveras, who art composed of the essence of thousands of Varunas, who art effulgent with the effulgence of thousands of moons, who art mightier than thousands of planets and thousands of Rudras, art hymnised by thousands of Brahmas and meditated upon by thousands of Rudras, and looked up to by thousands of Indras, and dost snap the chords of thousands of rebirths and unfetter the chains of thousands of bondage: dreadful as thousands of winds thou dost compassion to thousands of Indras.

SUTA SAID:—Having thus hymnised the Nrisinha-shaped Hari, the god Shiva, devoutly bent down, addressed him as follows:—

SHIVA SAID:—The Mātrikās, whom I had created for the purpose of killing the demon, Andhaka, are now devouring the inmates of the universe without paying heed to my admonition. Invincible though I am, yet I do not wish to kill them myself, as it is I who have brought them into being. How can I wish their annihilation, when I am their creator ?

SUTA SAID:—Having been thus addressed by Rudra, the lord (Nrisinha) caused the Mātrikās to be merged in his person, and having reestablished peace in this world, vanished in the air. The self-controlled votary, who reads this hymn to Nrisinha, is enabled, like Rudra, to witness the realisation of his desires. "I meditate upon Nrisinha, whose eyes are like the rising sun, and tongues of blazing fire are emitted from whose lotus-white mouth. I meditate upon the endless, originless Nrisinha, the original subjectivity, the most excellent lord of the universe and its final refuge." Recitation of this hymn by a person dissipates his misery as the sun destroys the dews. The Mātrikās fly the presence of such a person, and the god Hara waits upon him to do him a good turn. The destroyer of Tripura (Shiva) first promulgated the worship of Nrisinha, the lord of the gods, in this world, and was enabled to protect its inmates from the depredations of the Mātrikās, through his grace.

XLIV

THE JNANAMRITAM STOTRAM

Suta said:-

Now I shall narrate to you the hymns of the knowledge of ambrosia as the god Hara, interrogated by Nārada, first disclosed to him.

Narada said:- He, who is bound by the pairs of opposite, by anger and passion, by good and evil, by objects of the senses, is veritably an evil-minded and tyrannised being. O thou destroyer of Tripura, do I wish to learn from thee, the means of sailing across the sea of existence. Hearing this word of Nārada, Shambhu, the three-eyed deity, with his countenance beaming with joy. replied as follows:-

Maheshvara said:- Hear me, O thou foremost of the Rishis, the extremely secret hymn of Jnanamritam, which dissipates all misery and dispels the fear of chains of rebirths. He, through whose illusion all the inmates of the universe, from the humblest animalculum to the four-faced Brahmā, are enveloped in a delusive sleep of Nescience; if through the grace of such Vishnu one quits his sleep (delusion) and wakes the wakening of perfect knowledge, verily he liberates himself from the chain of necessary rebirths, so difficult of achievement even by the gods. Indifferent to cultivation of the knowledge of the Real, an individualised Self (man), introxicated with the wine of power, pride and luxury, sinks down, like a cow, in the oozy mire of worldliness. Fondly attached to their sons, wives and relations, men sink in the ocean of worldliness, as old and worn out wild elephants are drowned in one and the same ocean through an unconquerable instinct of companionship. I do not find the emancipation of that foolish person, even in the course of a hundred millions of re-births, who, like a silk-worm, imprisons his self in a cocoon of delusion. Hence, O Nārada, constantly meditate upon the self of Vishnu, the undecaying god of the gods, the lord of the universe, and worship him with the greatest self-control. He, who contemplates the birthless, originless, endless, omniscient, unmoving, all-pervading spirit, contained within its own self, is liberated from the trammels of life. He, who constantly contemplates the eternal Vishnu, the only reality that is unknowable, and which is without any parts (indivisible) and affections, lying beyond the sphere of mortality, the embodiment of sacrifice, the manifest and unmanifest, is liberated from the trammels of life. He, who contemplates the eternal, blissful, occult, all-seeing Vishnu, the infinite reality, devoid of all qualities, beyond all Nescience, is liberated from the trammels of life. He, who constantly meditates upon the disembodied, immoveable, omniscient, all-pervading Vishnu, the ordainer, the enjoyer of thoughts and sentiments, becomes an emancipated self. He, who constantly contemplates the lord Vishnu, who knows without the aid of sensations, who is unmanifest and without any substitute, and lies beyond the sphere of illusion, unaffected by disease or affection, the god Vāsudeva, the preceptor of all, is liberated from the trammels of life. He, who constantly contemplates the birthless Vishnu, the pure and perfect knowledge, which cannot be known by the senses, whom the mind comprehendeth not, and the speech fails to describe, the one unconquerable entity, is liberated from the trammels of life. He, who constantly contemplates Vishnu, who is without any limitation, mind, and sense of egoism, and is not affected by the pairs of opposite, is liberated from the trammels of life. He, who constantly contemplates the eternal, birthless, deathless, decayless, fearless Vishnu, that suffers no change, and has sprung from no seed, is liberated from the trammels of life. He, who constantly contemplates the great Vishnu, the deathless spirit, the infinite joy whom sin touches not and the senses cannot reach, is liberated from the trammels of life. He, who constantly contemplates the great Vishnu, devoid of good and evil, free from the dashings of the six kinds of waves (propulsions of the senses), the only knowable, sinless entity, is liberated from the trammels of life. He, who with undisturbed mind contemplates Vishnu, the embodiment of self, whose determination (cogitation) is truth, and whose seat is purity, is liberated from the trammels of life. He, who constantly contemplates the most excellent Vishnu, the lord of the universe, the knower of past, present, and future, the witness to whatever takes place in the universe, and who is beyond all speech (description), becomes an emancipated self. He, who constantly contemplates Vishnu, that lies beyond the ken of knowledge, the undecaying, eternal subjectivity, is liberated from the trammels of life. He, who constantly contemplates Vishnu, the protector of the universe, the friend, the grantor of all desired objects, the spirit that occupies the three regions and is imaged in the universe, is liberated from the trammels of life. He, who constantly contemplates Vishnu, the dissipator of all misery, the grantor of all bliss the extinguisher of all sin, is liberated from the trammels of life. He, who constantly contemplates Vishnu, who is always served by the Devas, Gandharvas, Apsarasas, Siddhas, Chāranas, Munis, and Yogins, is liberated from the trammels of life. He, who wishing to be liberated from the bond of existence constantly contemplates Vishnu by hymnising him in the abovesaid way, becomes a liberated self. The universe is established in Vishnu, Vishnu is established in the universe; he, who constantly contemplates the birthless Vishnu, the lord of the universe, is liberated from the trammels of life.

SUTA SAID:- The bull ensigned deity thus addressed the holy Narada of yore. I have narrated to you (the hymn) exactly as Shiva narrated it to that holy sage. O my child, by thus meditating upon the changeless, indivisible Brahma, you shall attain his eternal Self. The merit of celebrating a thousand horse-sacrifices and a hundred Vājapeya Yajnas does not rank a sixteenth part of what is acquired by meditating, for a moment, with undivided attention, on the eternal Self of Vishnu. The celestial Rishi (sage) having learnt from Ishvara (Shiva) of the superiority of Vishnu to all the gods devoutly worshipped him and attained to the region of Vishnu. He, who recites this excellent hymn, or hears it recited by others, stand absolved of sin, committed by him in the course of a million re-births. He, who, in a devout spirit, recites this hymn of Vishnu, narrated by Mahādeva, comes by immortality.

XLV

THE HYMN TI VISNU COMPOSED BY THE HOLY MÁRKANDEYA

Suta said:—

I shall narrate to you that hymn of Vishnu, which was first sung by the holy Mārkandeya. I lie prostrate before the thousand-eyed, lotus-navelled Nārāyana, the original being who is also addressed as Hrishikesha, what shall Death do unto me? I have placed myself under the protection of the birthless, undecaving, lotus-eyed Keshava, who pervades this universe; what shall Death do unto me? I crave the protection of the wielder of discus and conch-shell, the deity manifest in the shape of the visible universe, who may be perceived only with the inner sense; what shall Death do unto me? I have placed myself under the protection of the boar, dwarf, and Nrishinha manifestations of Vishnu, I crave the mercy of Mādhava and of Janārdana, what shall Death do unto me? I have surrendered myself to the mercy of the lord of the universe, the pure, eternal subject that manifests itself as the Ego in self-conscious individuals; what shall Death do unto me? I crave the protection of the wielder of discus and conch-shell, the deity manifest in the shape of this visible universe, who may be perceived only with the inner sense; what shall Death do unto me ? I have placed myself under the protection of the boar, dwarf and Nrisinha manifestations of Vishnu, I crave the mercy of Mādhava, and of Janārdana, what shall Death do unto me ? I have surrendered myself to the mercy of the lord of the universe, the pure, eternal subject that manifests itself as the Ego in self-conscious individuals, what shall Death do unto me ? I have surrendered myself to the protection of the thousand-headed, eternal reality, the great Yoga that is both manifest and unmanifest; what shall Death do unto me ? I have resigned myself to the care of the Supreme Self, the soul of all creatures, the one manifest in the shape of the universe, the one, that without taking birth in any womb, is incarnated through the merit of a religious sacrifice; what shall Death do unto me?

The god of Death, hearing this hymn of the Lord recited by Mārkandeya, hastily fled away chased by the emissaries of Vishnu. Thus the holy Mārkandeya conquered Death, nothing is rare to one with whom Nrisinha is pleased, impossibilities may happen even if the Lord wills it so. This death-dissolving hymn was first narrated by Vishnu to the holy Mārkandeya for his benefit. He, who recites this hymn, thrice every day, in a pure and devout spirit, suffers no premature death—a devotee of the undecaying one dies not an early death. Pondering within the lotus of his heart the god Nārāyana, the eternal, infinite, original subjectivity, more effulgent than the midday sun, the Rishi (Mārkandeya) was enabled to conquer death.

XLVI

THE HYMN TO ACHYUTA

SUTA SAID:-

O Shaunaka, now hear me narrate the hymn to the decay less one (Achyuta), which grant to its reciter all that he may wish to obtain, and which Brahmā being asked by Nārada first related to him.

NARADA SAID:—Be pleased to describe to me, O lord the undecaying, unchanging Vishnu, the grantor of all bliss who should be hymnised, every day, at the time of divine worship. Commendable and well-born are they, and they have achieved the end of their existence, who constantly hymnise the undecaying Vishnu. Such men are competent to confer all sorts of happiness on their kindred.

BRAHMA, SAID:—Hear me narrate, O holy age, the hymn to Vāsudeva, which grants emancipation to its reciters, and which, being sung at the time of worship by a votary, brings about the gratification of the deity. Om, obeisace to the god, Vāsudeva, the absolver of all sin, obeisance to the pure-bodied one, the embodiment of pure knowledge, obeisance to the lord of all the gods, who wears the ringlets of hair on his breast known as the Shrivatsa. Obeisance to the wielder of sword and buckle, who wears a garland of lotus flowers around his neck. Obeisance to the mainstay of the universe, to the support of the heaven-to the dreadful Nrisinha (Man-lion), to the light that burns in the heart, free from doubt and hesitation (Vaikuntha). Obeisance to the lotus-navelled, thousand-headed one, who lies on the serpent of eternity (Shesha) in the ocean of the milk of ambrosia (Kshiroda). Obeisance to the destroyer of the Kshatriya race, who wields a battle-axe in his hand. Obeisance, over and again, to the adorable and the true-willed one. Obeisance to the lord of the three regions, to the discus-wielding divinity, to the subtlest, original, blissful principle. Obeisance to the dwarf-shaped god, who relieved Vali of the cares of a kingdom-to the spirit of the sacrifice, manifest in the shape of the primordial boar. Om obeisance to Govinda. Obeisance to the highest joy, to the perfect knowledge to one who is eternal knowledge and oridinal idea and from whom all knowledge proceeds. Obeisance to the supreme, secondless reality, to the foremost subjectivity, to the creator, governor and final cause of the universe, to the fountain sources of all knowledge, to the supreme idealist whose idea has taken shape in the form of the universe. Obeisance to the destroyer of Madhu (amativeness), to the killer of Rāvana, and to the god who brought about the ruins of the demons Kansa, Keshi and Kaitabha. Obeisance to the lotus-eyed one, to the Garuda-ensigned divinity, to the destroyer of Kālanemi, to the one that rides on the pinions of the celestial Garuda. Obeisance to the son of Devaki, to the joy of the race of Vrishni, to the lord of Rukmini, to the son of Aditi. Obeisance to the Gokula-abiding one, to the darling of Goclula, to Krishna, the darling of the milk-maids. Victory to the wielder of the mount Govardhana, to the killer of Vāna, to the destroyer of Chānur and Kāliva; victory to the eternal truth the eternal witness of the universal phenomena, to the fulfiller of all ends, to the all-giving Mādhava known only by the Vādāntins. Victory to the unmanifest, occult, undecaying reality, that runs through all to perfect knowledge, to the undecaying self of supreme felicity. Victory to the self of eternal peace that is without support (does not depend on any thing), to the adorable Vishnu, the lord of the universe.

Thou art the preceptor, the disciple, the initiation, and the mystic formula. Thou art the Nyāsa (psychic location or projection), the rules, postures, and Mudrās of Yoga; thou, art the implements of worship such as flowers, offerings, etc. Thou art the supreme receptivity, the mystic tortoise, the emblem of the pendency of the world; thou art the mystic lotus, the sacrificial platform and the deities that preside over the mystic diagram (Mandalam) such as, the energies of virtue, knowledge, etc. Thou art Rama, the wielder of the plough-share, the destroyer of Samvara; thou art the Devas and the Brahmarshis, thou art the all-pervading god whose prowess is truth. Thou art the Adityas, Vasus, Rudras, Ashvis, Maruts, Devas, Dānavas, Nāgas, Yakshas, Rākshasas, and Khagas. Thou art the Gandharvas, Apsarasas, Siddhas, Pitris, and the immortals. Thou art the universal matter, the senses, the unmanifest one; thou art the mind, intellect, egoism, objects of sense-perception, and the self-conscious ego, the god that resides in the hearts of all creatures. Thou art the sacrifice, the implements of sacrifice, the sacrificial Mantras, the oblations, the priest, the sacrificer, the chanter of the Vedic Mantras, the burnt offering, the priest that casts the sacrifical animal in fire. Thou art the firmament with its suns and starry constellations, the nether regions, the universal expanse of ether, the region of Maha; in short whatever is found to exist among men, beast and Devas, all creation whether mobile or immobile are but the manifestations of thy eternal Self, O Lord. Who can behold thy eternal and universal image, O Lord, which can not be perceived by the senses, which is invisible to the immortals, and which only the Yogins behold in their psychic trance? Who can comprehend thy real, unmanifest, birthless, deathless, changeless, undecaying, all-pervading, perfect, secondless Self, which is infinite reality, perfect purity, pure knowledge, though devoid of qualities and full of supreme felicity ? The shape which thou assumest in any particular incarnation, any of them the Devas, in their limited capacity, meditate upon as a substitute for thy real Self. O thou, infinite subjectivity, how shall I be able to worship thy real Self, which the mind comprehendeth not and the senses do not perceive. I have been able to worship with offerings of flowers etc., only a few of thy attributes, O lord, manifest in the shape of Sankarsena, etc. Be graciously pleased to pardon me for the defects in my performance of Japas and Homas, as well as for any omission on my part in connection with thy divine worship. I have not been able to worship thee, O lord, as laid down in the Shāstras, with due devotion, so be pleased to pardon my inefficiency. Day and night, morning and evening, whether moving or at rest, my devotion is firmly attached to thy feet, O lord. I do not care for my body, I am quite indifferent to the performances of religious rites, my sole delight is in thee O lord of the universe. What has he not done for the attainment of heaven, or for self-emancipation, who has placed a firm faith in Vishnu, the grantor of all desires ? Who is there in the universe, who can worship or hymnise thee to the fullest extent ? Be pleased to accept this humble and deficient worship which I have made of thee, to-day.

Thus I have narrated to you, O sage, the hymn to the discus-wielding deity; sing his glories in a devout spirit, if you wish to attain the supreme bliss. He, who recites this hymn at the close of a worship of the universal preceptor, is able to work out his salvation in no time, and becomes freed from the bonds of re-births. Even in the Kali Yuga he, who recites this hymn, thrice, every day, in a pure spirit, obtains all that he, wishes to obtain. By reading this hymn to Vishnu, a sonless man obtains a son, a sick person gets rid of disease, an indigent man obtains wealth, a captive obtains his liberty, a seeker after erudition obtains erudition, a seeker after fame obtains renown, even the remembrances of his part births recur to a man who recites this hymn. He, who sings the glories of the absolute subjectivity, is truly wise, is really pure and truthful in his speech. He is omniscient and acquires the merit of performing all the religious rites. Those, who are not propelled to do any thing for the service of Hari (God), or are not fondly moved towards him, are beyond the pale of all religion. No purificatory rite can purify the mind or speech of the miscreant, who has not an unswerving faith in the all-pervading lord (Vishnu). By duly worship the god Hari, the grantor of all comforts, a person obtains whatever he wishes to obtain in this life, I make obeisance to the immortal, birthless, all-pervading god, who resides in the hearts of all creature, and whom the Asuras, Siddhas, and erudite persons can not comprehend in their minds, whom only the holy sages know, and who is the sole witness of the universal phenomena. I make offerings of the flowers of sentiments, of pure, pleasurable faith and love to the eternal, universal lord, the embodiment of self, devoid of all qualities, the absolute purity: may that all-witnessing Self, the perfect knowledge, reside in my heart.

Thus I have narrated to you the hymn to the endless, originless supreme Vishnu. Let a man, whose mind is shorn of all desires, constantly meditate upon his divine self, in as much as he is the god. Where is the Yogin who by contemplating the pure, original, secondless subjectivity, effulgent as the sun, is not merged in his eternal essence ? The self-controlled person, who recites this hymn in a devotional spirit, becomes absolved of all sin, and enters the infinite region presided over by Murāri. He, who prays for friendship of the god, as well as for liberation of self, and virtue, and object of desire is freed from all the shackles of life, and attains Vishnu, the adorable refuge of all. He, who abjuring all company takes recourse to Vādudeva, the absolute purity, the lord, the governor and destroyer of the universe, is freed from the shackles of life, and becomes an emancipated self.